# Betty Crocker's

# FAMILY DINNERS In a Hurry

Director of Photography:
STEPHEN MANVILLE

 **Golden Press • New York**

Western Publishing Company, Inc.
Racine, Wisconsin

*Pictured on cover:*
Pepper Steak [page 78].

Fourth Printing, 1973
Copyright © 1970 by General Mills, Inc., Minneapolis, Minnesota.
All rights reserved. Produced in the U.S.A. Library of Congress
Catalog Card Number: 78-112874

Dear Friend,

Much as you may love to cook, your time in the kitchen is usually limited. What with a club meeting, a job or any morning's list of things-to-be-done-today, you're lucky to have an hour of pre-dinner kitchen time. But a busy day for you needn't mean a catch-as-catch-can dinner for the family. Today, with thousands of packaged, canned and frozen foods, plus the added convenience of small appliances, meals that once took hours to prepare can be turned out in a matter of minutes. All you need are some guidelines to point the way. And that's what this book is all about.

Here are 45 when-time-counts menus that cater to a wide variety of tastes—from small-fry favorites to dishes Dad especially likes. In addition to the family-tested recipes, each menu offers its own timetable for preparation, and one or more timesaving shortcuts. (Many even have market lists to speed your shopping.) And all of these recipes have been tested by busy women like you all over the country.

We hope that this book will help you to enjoy your many activities, confident that a delicious dinner is never more than an hour away.

Yours in haste,

Betty Crocker

# Contents

# Making the Minutes Count

*Double-quick cooking methods almost make a game of getting these meals on the table. With fluster-proof planning, you just can't miss. What's the secret? Timesaving shortcuts, a little creativity and up-to-date, itemized lists of packaged, canned and frozen foods you'll want to have on hand at all times.*

Once upon a time, woman's place was in the home. Today, with so many activities to occupy a homemaker's day, we realize that the time left for preparing the family meals is at a premium. What is needed are quick, easy-to-make dinners that can go from kitchen to table in an hour at most.

Quick meals, however, come in many guises. There's the kind made by opening a can, warming the contents and setting it before a long-suffering family. And then there's the kind that is a *real* dinner—attractive, wholesome and delicious—a dinner that looks and tastes as if it had taken hours to prepare instead of a few minutes. That is the only kind of hurry-up meal we think merits discussion. And how to achieve it is what this book is all about.

Since the best place to begin anything is at the beginning, we'll begin by pointing out that you cannot prepare any kind of meal in a hurry if you do not have the necessary supplies on hand, in the house, at the time you want to use them. So, Rule No. 1 is:

**Plan ahead.** Know what you want to serve, what foods you will need and have them within easy reach when you begin to prepare the meal. And don't trust to luck that your supply of staples, seasonings and other basic foodstuffs is adequate. Be sure. Each week, check your kitchen shelves, your refrigerator, your freezer. If any item is running low, make a note and replace it *before* it runs out, not after.

Next, plan your menus for the entire week—the complete menu, not just the main dish. Vary the menus by serving potatoes one day, rice the next, noodles on the third day. Do the same with vegetables. Give them a new look by combining two, i.e., carrots and lima beans. Toss some sliced zucchini into a green salad for new flavor. Add a dash of instant onion to baked squash for a little crunch. The possibilities are endless.

Also, if you decide to have a roast on Sunday, plan right then when and how you will use the leftover meat. Instead of a repeat performance the next night, fix an altogether different dish for Monday, then bring on the leftover roast in a new form on the following night. As an example, the Pork Loin Roast on page 31 will be greeted with a lot more enthusiasm if it appears the second time around as Pork Chow Mein (page 72) or Pork and Stuffing Bake (page 86). Other menus in this book have been planned with leftovers in mind, too.

All right—pencil in hand, you are ready to make out your market list. Want a tip? Shop once for the week and group all of the items according to their location in your supermarket. It saves backtracking, extra footsteps and, even more important, precious time. If it's at all possible, do your shopping when the store is least likely to be crowded but when you can still take advantage of any advertised specials. It's a good time to compare prices and to discover new products.

When you return from the market laden with the makings of a week's family meals, you are ready for Rule No. 2:

**Prepare ahead.** Wash the salad greens and other fresh vegetables, then refrigerate in plastic bags or the crisper. Shape ground beef into patties, stack them with double thicknesses of freezer wrap between and freeze. And, while you're at it, pick over cherries or grapes and store them in a fruit bowl that can go directly to the table. The fruit makes an attractive centerpiece or an easy dessert—or both. The time it takes to do these things now will be time you'll save before dinner. And one more thing: Whenever feasible, cook ahead or freeze ahead for future use. If certain dishes are family favorites you are likely to serve often, make a double or triple batch (e.g., meat loaf, chili, lasagne) and freeze. Bake an extra layer cake or a second pie shell and have it waiting in the freezer. One of the very best timesavers along this line is our Quantity Make-ahead Meatballs on page 13. They're featured in three recipes in this book (on pages 12, 26 and 39) and we know you'll find ways to use them in your own recipes.

So, here you are—all set to whip up any of these meals and whisk them onto the table in a jiffy. You've planned your menus for the week, done the shopping and prepared as much ahead as you could. Is there anything else you can do that will save time? Yes, there is. Take a look around your kitchen. Now that *you* are organized for fast action, is *it* organized to help you? Are the saucepans near the range, within easy reach? Is mixing equipment close to the work counter? No one expects you to rebuild your kitchen, but you'll be surprised at how many steps a rearranging of equipment can save. How about equipment—knives sharp, pans in tip-top shape, anything that should be replaced? It's better to take care of it now than have it break down just when you need it most.

Up to this point, we've been concerned with getting you ready to use this book. Now for a word as to how this book is organized.

Still with an eye to time as an all-important factor in your life, we have grouped these hurry-up dinners according to the length of time needed to prepare them. Beginning with the speediest (15 to 25 minutes), they range all the way to a maximum of 50 to 60 minutes. And we've condensed the wording in the Timetable for fast reading. When we tell you to cook noodles so many minutes, we've allowed for the time it takes to heat water to boiling as well as the actual cooking time.

Our salad-making time presupposes that you've followed our earlier suggestion, so that the greens are already washed and chilled. We haven't detailed such minor tasks as putting the bread, butter and relishes on the table, and have chosen not to clutter up the market lists with staples. Once you have mastered the technique of putting a meal together quickly, you'll probably find yourself substituting or switching menus around.

There'll be times when you'll want to add a first course—maybe mugs of steaming soup or glasses of chilled fruit juice or a tray of crisp relishes. And you might decide to serve a favorite green salad instead of the one we suggest in a particular menu. Fine. We expect you to. Just remember to make adequate allowance in the Timetable for any time difference in preparation and make sure that your change or substitution doesn't affect the nutritional balance of the meal.

One final word. An attractive setting for a dinner is like the right frame for a work of art. *Your* work of art deserves a setting that will make it look just as good as it tastes. So set a cheerful table. Have two or three sets of plastic place mats (so easy to wipe clean!) and interchange them in different color combinations.

7

*Do* have a centerpiece; it needn't be elaborate. A flourishing green plant, a bowl of fresh fruit or a basket of freshly scrubbed vegetables, flowers from your own garden, even something one of the children made in school.

*Do* be ready at the drop of a hat to move the dinner onto the patio on a warm summer evening or in front of the fire on a cold winter night. And, just for the fun of it, surprise the family every now and then with candlelight. Even a simple meal will seem like a banquet.

We have saved any listings until last. We think you'll find them useful, so much so that you may want to copy the checklists for staples and other Nice-to-Have's and stick them to the inside of your cupboard door.

Throughout the book, you'll find timesaving tricks and easy ways of preparation, all with one thing in mind—to save *you* time. In addition, we think you'll find that the following general tips and lists are useful guidelines for any hurry-up meal.

# Basic Tips for Meals on Time

**1.** Read through the menu to familiarize yourself with it; assemble all the ingredients and equipment you are going to need.

**2.** Place cans of fruit and vegetables for salads in refrigerator ahead of time for chilling or, if a quick-chill is necessary, put cans in the freezer while you're preparing the meal.

**3.** Use kitchen scissors to snip parsley or to cut marshmallows and dried fruit, as well as other ingredients that take time to chop.

**4.** When heating water for noodles or frozen vegetables, start with hot tap water.

**5.** Use cookware that goes from oven-to-freezer-to-oven-to-table. Or freeze in a casserole, then remove frozen contents and wrap in foil so casserole is available for use. When you're ready to heat, just pop the frozen block into the same casserole.

**6.** Use plastic pop-out ice cube trays to freeze bouillon, chicken broth, etc., then store cubes in moisture-vapor-proof plastic bag.

**7.** Bake double batches of cookies and freeze one batch for use later. The same can be done with cakes and pies. Pastry dough can be rolled out, cut into squares and frozen to use for tart shells as in the Baked Fish Dinner (page 88).

**8.** Freeze chopped onion and chopped green pepper for quick use later on. Or substitute instant onion and dehydrated pepper flakes.

**9.** Serve desserts that bake or chill while the main course is being prepared and served. And use the quick-set trick described on page 73 when making gelatin salads and desserts.

**10.** Let the children help. They can set the table, fill glasses, make salads, etc.

**11.** For a quick garnish that makes meals more attractive and fun, keep on hand items such as maraschino cherries, parsley, olives and chopped nuts. (And have you ever tried carrot tops or celery leaves for a speedy garnish?)

**12.** If possible, clean up as you work, washing cooking equipment or soaking it in water.

## "Must" Items to Have on Hand:

### STAPLES
flour
buttermilk baking mix
cornstarch
sugar ( granulated, brown,
    confectioners' )
shortening
salad oil
instant rice
spaghetti, macaroni and noodles
bottled salad dressings
vinegar
bottled lemon juice
vanilla
lemon and almond extracts
Worcestershire sauce
instant beef and chicken bouillon
    or bouillon cubes
instant minced onion
parsley flakes
mustard
catsup
coffee
tea

### SEASONINGS
allspice
basil leaves
chili powder
cinnamon
dill weed
garlic salt
ginger
dry mustard
nutmeg
oregano
paprika
pepper
salt
savory
seasoned salt
thyme

## Good "Extras" to Keep on Hand:

### IN THE CUPBOARD (canned)
Meats: tuna, salmon, luncheon meat, ham
Assortment of canned soups
Assortment of canned fruits and vegetables
Miscellaneous:
    ready-to-serve sauces
    ready-to-serve puddings
    pie fillings (cherry, apple, blueberry)
    ready-to-spread frostings
    mushrooms
    peanut butter

### IN THE CUPBOARD (packaged)
soup, sauce, gravy and salad dressing
    mixes
flavored gelatins (several flavors)
cake mixes (several flavors)
dessert mixes and toppings
muffin mixes
pie crust mix
casserole mixes (scalloped and au gratin
    potatoes, rice and noodle mixes)
instant mashed potato puffs
instant nonfat dry milk
herbed croutons
dry bread crumbs
graham crackers and/or crumbs
grated Parmesan cheese

### IN THE FREEZER
Assortment of fruits and vegetables
Meats: cubed steaks, ground beef,
    turkey roast
Miscellaneous:
    frozen whipped topping
    fruit juices
    cake, waffles, ice cream, sherbet

### IN THE REFRIGERATOR
butter or margarine
milk
eggs
lettuce

# MAKING THE MINUTES COUNT

## Recommended Utensils for Your Kitchen:

FOR PREPARATION
- electric mixer
- toaster
- cutting board
- cutlery set (chef's knife, 7 or 8"
  blade; serrated knife;
  2 paring knives)
- mixing bowls (convenient sizes)
- strainer (medium mesh, medium size)
- colander
- can opener
- bottle and jar opener
- wooden spoons
- slotted spoon
- rubber scraper
- rotary beater
- spatulas
- long-handled fork
- tongs
- kitchen scissors
- vegetable brush
- vegetable parer
- grater or shredder
- pastry blender
- rolling pin and cover
- pastry cloth
- refrigerator and freezer containers

FOR MEASURING
- 1 set nested dry measuring cups
- liquid measuring cup
- 1 set measuring spoons

FOR TOP-OF-THE-RANGE COOKING
- skillets with covers (6 and 10 or 12")
- saucepans with covers
  (1-, 2- and 4- or 6-qt.)

FOR BAKING
- cutter for cookies and biscuits
- baking pan (13x9x2")
- bread loaf pan (9x5x3")
- baking sheet (without sides)
- muffin pan (6 or 12 cups)
- pie pans (8 and 9")
- 2 round layer pans (9")
- square pans (8x8x2 and 9x9x2")
- wire cooling racks
- casseroles with covers (1-, 1½- and 2-qt.)
- 6 custard cups
- pot holders

NICE TO HAVE
- thermometers (oven, meat, candy, deep fat)
- kitchen timer
- wire whisk
- tube pan (10x4" deep)
- jelly roll pan (15½x10½x1")
- roasting pan (with rack)
- Dutch oven
- electric skillet (10- or 12-inch)
- pressure cooker (4- or 6-quart)
- blender
- knife sharpener
- food chopper or grinder
- griddle
- soufflé dish
- gelatin molds
- melon ball cutter
- lemon squeezer

And now, on your way—to the kitchen, that is! You are about to prove to your hungry horde that a day out of the house for you doesn't mean cold cuts for them.

# 15- to 25-Minute Dinners

*Emergencies do happen. Busy days do overflow with unexpected activities. But no matter, the family must still be fed every day. Even with a late, late start, however, you can work wonders with a well-stocked cupboard and freezer—and these appetizing menus.*

# Freezer Fast

*Nothing beats the convenience of the one-dish meal that goes direct from range to table. In this one, savory meatballs are baked ahead of time, then stored in the freezer until needed. The frozen vegetables and meatballs simmer in separate sections of the skillet and are ready to eat in 20 minutes. An electric skillet makes things even simpler; the main course can be prepared right at the table. At serving time, English muffins pop into the toaster on demand while Chocolate Banana Bobs wait in the refrigerator. The biggest plus of all? The meatballs can be made in quantity and stored for use in other recipes. They'll keep in the freezer up to 2 months.*

*Meatball Vegetable Medley*
*Toasted English Muffins*
*Chocolate Banana Bobs*
*Milk    Coffee*

---

### TIMETABLE

**Ahead of time:**
  Prepare meatballs; freeze
  Prepare Chocolate Banana Bobs; freeze
**25 minutes before:**
  Prepare and cook Meatball Vegetable Medley
**10 minutes before:**
  Set table
**Just before serving:**
  Cut muffins in half; toast in toaster or broiler
  Remove banana bobs from freezer to thaw slightly
**Serve dinner.**

## MEATBALL VEGETABLE MEDLEY

*Pictured on preceding page.*

- 1 can (10½ ounces) condensed cream of mushroom soup
- ½ cup milk
- 1 package (9 ounces) frozen French-style green beans
- 1 package (10 ounces) frozen whole kernel corn
- 1 recipe Make-ahead Meatballs (right)

In large skillet, stir together soup and milk. Place frozen blocks of beans and corn in separate sections of skillet. Add meatballs to skillet. Cover; heat to boiling over medium heat. Reduce heat to low; cover and cook 5 minutes. Break vegetables apart with fork (do not stir together); cover and cook 5 minutes longer or until heated through.

*4 servings.*

**Note:** If using electric skillet, set control at 400° to heat to boiling, then reduce heat to 300° to finish cooking.

## MAKE-AHEAD MEATBALLS

1 pound ground beef
3 tablespoons instant minced onion
½ cup dry bread crumbs
1 teaspoon salt
⅛ teaspoon pepper
½ teaspoon Worcestershire sauce
1 egg
¼ cup milk

Heat oven to 400°. Mix all ingredients thoroughly. Shape mixture into 1-inch balls. Place in ungreased jelly roll pan, 15½x10½x1 inch. Bake about 10 minutes or until done.

To freeze, cool meatballs about 5 minutes. Place in freezer 15 minutes. Pack partially frozen meatballs in freezer container, heavy plastic bag or wrap securely in aluminum foil. Label, date and place in freezer.

*About 35 meatballs.*

## QUANTITY MAKE-AHEAD MEATBALLS

*Make this quantity recipe and keep these meatballs on hand for freezer-fast meals. Other menus featuring Make-ahead Meatballs are Soup-bowl Stew (page 26) and Meatballs Romanoff (page 39).*

3 pounds ground beef
⅓ cup instant minced onion
1½ cups dry bread crumbs
1 tablespoon salt
¼ teaspoon pepper
1½ teaspoons Worcestershire sauce
3 eggs
¾ cup milk

Make and freeze meatballs as directed above except—place one third of meatballs in each of 3 containers.

*Three 1-quart freezer containers (35 meatballs each).*

## CHOCOLATE BANANA BOBS

2 medium bananas
2 tablespoons shortening
6 bars (¾ ounce each) milk chocolate
  candy (plain or with crisped rice)

Peel bananas and cut each into four to six 1½- to 2-inch pieces. Insert wooden ice-cream stick in each piece; place on baking sheet. Freeze until bananas are firm, about 2 hours.

In small saucepan, melt shortening and chocolate candy over low heat, stirring occasionally. Dip banana pieces into chocolate, quickly spreading mixture completely over pieces. Place on baking sheet covered with waxed paper; freeze until firm.

When firm, wrap each in aluminum foil and place in freezer. Remove from freezer 15 minutes before serving.

*8 to 12 banana bobs.*

### Market List

1 can (10½ ounces) condensed cream of
  mushroom soup
6 bars (¾ ounce each) milk chocolate
  candy (plain or with crisped rice)
  English muffins
2 bananas
1 package (9 ounces) frozen French-style
  green beans
1 package (10 ounces) frozen whole
  kernel corn

# Hurry-up Hospitality

*"Can Susan stay for supper?" If your youngsters are given to issuing last-minute invitations, rely on a well-stocked freezer for most of the meal. Here's just such a menu, bound to rate raves from the junior contingent. The main course is an adaptation of a French dip—steak sandwiches to dunk in bowls of savory gravy. Prepare the dessert while the children clear the table. It's a sure child-pleaser that tops cake with candy, candy with marshmallows, and broils for a mere minute. Susan's mother is certain to hear about this meal.*

*Dip 'n Dunk Steak Sandwiches*
*Two-tone Beans*
*Cherry Tomatoes and Green Onions*
*Toasted Cake S'mores*
*Milk   Coffee*

---

### TIMETABLE

**Ahead of time:**
  Wash onions and tomatoes; refrigerate
**20 minutes before:**
  Set table
  Prepare bread
  Cook beans
  Arrange tomatoes and onions in serving
    dishes
**10 minutes before:**
  Panfry cube steaks (using 2 skillets
    speeds up the browning)
  Make gravy
  Toast bread
**Serve main course.**
**Arrange cake s'mores; broil and serve.**

14

## DIP 'N DUNK STEAK SANDWICHES

Panfry desired number frozen 2-ounce beef cube steaks over medium-high heat, turning to brown both sides. (If using 4-ounce beef minute steaks, melt 1 tablespoon shortening in skillet before cooking steaks.) Season with salt and pepper. Remove steaks; keep warm.

To make gravy, drain fat from skillet. For each serving pour about ⅓ cup water into skillet. Heat to boiling, scraping brown particles from bottom of skillet. For each cup of water, stir in ½ teaspoon seasoned salt or 1 teaspoon instant beef bouillon.

Place desired number of buttered ½-inch slices French bread or hamburger bun halves on ungreased baking sheet. If desired, sprinkle bread with garlic salt. Place on broiler rack about 4 inches from heat; toast until golden brown.

Place steaks between toasted bread slices; cut in half. Serve gravy in individual small bowls. Each person can "dunk" his sandwich, or pour gravy over it.

**Note:** Packaged frozen 2-ounce beef cube steaks are a handy convenience to have on hand any time.

Panfry cube steaks quickly; use a spatula to turn them.

Scrape brown particles from skillet when making gravy.

Toast slices of French bread until golden.

Toasted Cake S'mores

## TWO-TONE BEANS

1 package (9 ounces) frozen cut green
  beans
1 package (9 ounces) frozen cut wax
  beans
½ teaspoon savory
1 to 2 tablespoons butter or margarine

Cook beans as directed on package except—
use only the amount of water called for on
1 package. Drain; stir in savory and butter.

*6 servings.*

## CHERRY TOMATOES
## AND GREEN ONIONS

Wash and drain 1 pint cherry tomatoes (do
not remove stems). Clean 2 bunches green
onions (about 16), leaving 3-inch green stem
on each. Arrange tomatoes and onions in
serving dishes.

**16**   *6 servings.*

## CANDY S'MORES

6 slices cut from frozen pound cake
4 bars (¾ ounce each) milk chocolate
  candy
  Miniature marshmallows

Place cake slices on ungreased baking sheet.
Place 6 or 7 squares of candy on each slice.
Arrange marshmallows on candy.

Set oven control at broil and/or 550°. Broil
about 5 inches from heat about 1 minute or
until marshmallows are golden brown.

*6 servings.*

### VARIATION

■ *Toasted Cake S'mores:* Substitute 1 can (16.5
ounces) chocolate frosting for the candy;
spread 1 to 2 tablespoons frosting on each
cake slice.

French bread or hamburger buns
4 bars (¾ ounce each) milk chocolate candy
  Miniature marshmallows
2 bunches green onions
1 pint cherry tomatoes
1 package (9 ounces) frozen cut green beans
1 package (9 ounces) frozen cut wax beans
  Frozen beef cube steaks
  Frozen pound cake

# Straight from the Broiler

*Broiler cooking is too quick and easy to be confined to meat alone. So why not take advantage of these virtues for other foods as well? Here the broil-alongs with ham are pineapple slices and sweet potatoes with banana. Serve such meals straight from the broiler to warmed dinner plates—saves cleanup and helps keep the food hot. For dessert, mix peanut butter with chocolate syrup for a bound-to-be-popular ice-cream topping.*

---

*Broiled Ham and Pineapple Slices*
*Sweet Potatoes with Banana*
*Broccoli Spears with Lemon Butter*
*Rye Bread*
*Chocolate Peanut Butter Sundaes*
*Milk      Coffee*

---

## TIMETABLE

**25 minutes before:**
Set table
Prepare sauce for sundaes
Drain sweet potatoes and pineapple
**15 minutes before:**
Cook broccoli
Prepare ham
**About 11 minutes before:**
Broil ham
Prepare Sweet Potatoes with Banana; broil
**About 6 minutes before:**
Turn ham
Make lemon butter sauce
Top ham with pineapple slices
**Serve main course.**
**Prepare sundaes; serve.**

## BROILED HAM AND PINEAPPLE SLICES

**1- to 1½-pound ham slice, ½ inch thick**
**1 can (8½ ounces) sliced pineapple, drained (reserve syrup for sweet potatoes)**
**Soft butter or margarine**

Diagonally slash outer edge of fat on ham slice at 1-inch intervals to prevent curling. Set oven control at broil and/or 550°. Place ham on rack in broiler pan. Broil 3 inches from heat 5 minutes on each side or until light brown. During last 2 minutes of broiling, arrange pineapple slices on ham; brush slices with butter.

*4 servings.*

### VARIATIONS
■ *Orange-glazed Ham Slice:* Omit pineapple and butter; spread 3 tablespoons orange marmalade on ham slice after turning ham and during last 2 minutes of broiling.

■ *Mustard-glazed Ham Slice:* Omit pineapple and butter; mix 2 tablespoons brown sugar, 1 tablespoon prepared mustard and 1 to 2 teaspoons honey or corn syrup. Spread over ham slice after turning and during last 2 minutes of broiling.

17

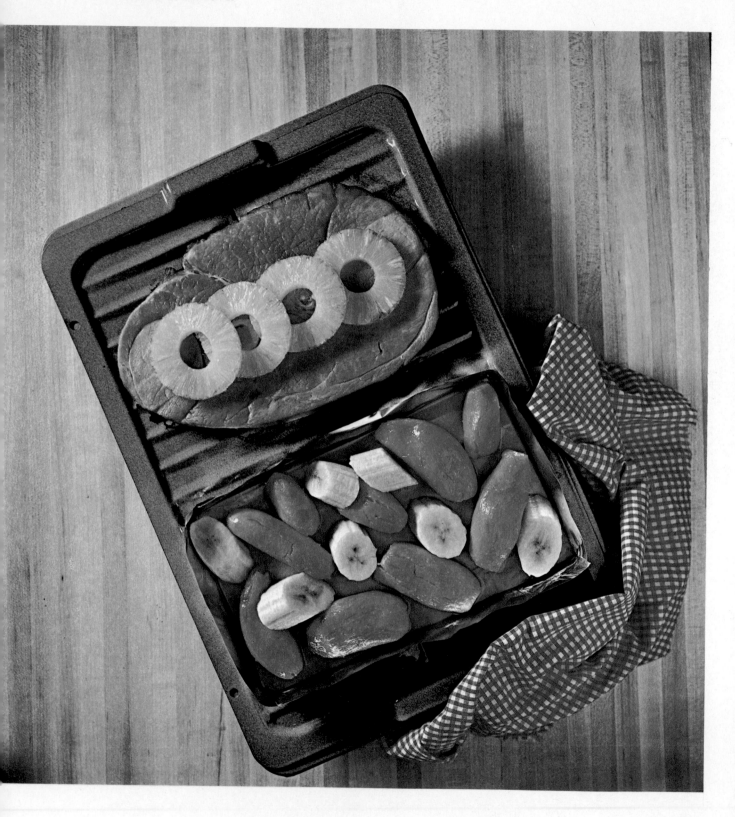

## SWEET POTATOES WITH BANANA

1 can (1 pound 7 ounces) vacuum-pack
   sweet potatoes
1 large banana
½ cup brown sugar (packed)
2 tablespoons soft butter or margarine
2 tablespoons reserved pineapple syrup
   or corn syrup
⅛ teaspoon salt

Shape aluminum foil into a broiler pan, 10x7x1½ inches. Drain sweet potatoes; arrange in foil pan. If potatoes are large, cut in half. Diagonally slice banana into pan.

Mix brown sugar, butter, pineapple syrup and salt; spoon over sweet potatoes and banana.

Set oven control at broil and/or 550°. Place foil pan on broiler rack; broil 3 inches from heat 5 to 8 minutes or until potatoes are hot.

*4 servings.*

## BROCCOLI SPEARS WITH LEMON BUTTER

2 packages (10 ounces each)
   frozen broccoli spears
2 tablespoons butter or margarine
1 tablespoon lemon juice

Cook broccoli spears as directed on package. Melt butter with lemon juice over low heat. Pour over hot broccoli.

*4 generous servings.*

### VARIATIONS

■ *Broccoli with Mustard Butter:* Decrease lemon juice to ½ teaspoon; add ⅛ teaspoon mustard and dash sugar and salt.

■ *Broccoli with Horseradish Butter:* Omit lemon juice and add 1½ teaspoons horseradish.

## CHOCOLATE PEANUT BUTTER SUNDAES

¼ cup peanut butter
½ cup chocolate syrup
1 pint vanilla ice cream

Blend peanut butter and chocolate syrup. Divide ice cream among 4 dessert dishes. Spoon sauce over ice cream.

*4 servings.*

### VARIATIONS

■ *Honey Peanut Butter Sundaes:* Substitute ½ cup honey for the chocolate syrup.

■ *Peanut Butter 'n Jelly Sundaes:* Substitute ¼ to ½ cup jelly for the chocolate syrup.

■ *Peanut Butterscotch Sundaes:* Substitute ¼ cup butterscotch ice-cream topping for the chocolate syrup.

Market List

1- to 1½-pound ham slice, ½ inch thick
1 can (8½ ounces) sliced pineapple
1 can (1 pound 7 ounces) vacuum-pack
   sweet potatoes
Chocolate syrup
Peanut butter
Rye bread
1 large banana
2 packages (10 ounces each) frozen broccoli
   spears
1 pint vanilla ice cream

19

# Bit o' Britain— Fish and Chips

*Borrow an idea from our English cousins and serve a supper of fish and chips that's a snap to prepare. Fifteen minutes is all it takes to broil frozen fish sticks and French fries, cook the spinach, slice and season the cucumbers and mix the cocktail sauce. To keep cleanup at a minimum, the fish sticks and French fries can go from broiler to plate along with the spinach; and the cocktail sauce can be served in little paper cups or poured over the fish sticks. For that special touch, why not serve the colorful bubbly dessert in your best glass dishes? It's a pretty ending to a delicious and satisfying meal.*

*Fish 'n Chips*
*Cocktail Sauce*
*Lemon-buttered Spinach*
*Cucumbers in Dilled Sour Cream*
*Sparkling Fruit*
*Milk       Coffee*

## TIMETABLE

**15 minutes before:**
  Make salad
  Make Cocktail Sauce
  Cook spinach
  Place fish sticks and potatoes in broiler pan
**10 minutes before:**
  Broil fish sticks and potatoes
  Set table
  Drain fruit
**Serve main course.**
**Prepare dessert; serve.**

20

## FISH 'N CHIPS

2 packages (8 ounces each) frozen fish sticks
1 package (1 pound) frozen French fried potatoes

Set oven control at broil and/or 550°. Place frozen fish sticks and frozen potatoes in single layer on rack in broiler pan, baking sheet or jelly roll pan, 15½x10½x1 inch. Broil 6 inches from heat about 8 minutes or until fish and potatoes are hot.

*4 servings.*

**Note:** If desired, substitute 2 packages (1 pound each) frozen English-style fish 'n chips for the fish sticks and potatoes. Follow package directions and adjust Timetable for the meal.

## COCKTAIL SAUCE

½ cup catsup
2 to 3 teaspoons horseradish
2 tablespoons lemon juice

Stir together all ingredients in small bowl.

*About ⅔ cup.*

## SPARKLING FRUIT

1 can (about 1 pound) fruit cocktail,
  drained
1 pint lemon or lime sherbet
1 bottle (7 ounces) carbonated
  lemon-lime beverage

At serving time, divide fruit cocktail among 4 dessert dishes. Top each with scoop of sherbet. Pour beverage over each serving.

*4 servings.*

### VARIATIONS

■ *Sparkling Peaches:* Omit fruit cocktail; substitute 1 can (1 pound) peaches, drained.

■ *Sparkling Pineapple:* Omit fruit cocktail; substitute 1 can (13½ ounces) pineapple tidbits, drained.

## LEMON-BUTTERED SPINACH

1 package (10 ounces) frozen chopped
  spinach
1 to 2 tablespoons butter or margarine
1 tablespoon lemon juice

Cook spinach as directed on package. Drain; stir in butter and lemon juice.

*4 servings.*

**Note:** If your family is particularly fond of spinach, use 2 packages in the above recipe.

## CUCUMBERS IN DILLED SOUR CREAM

1 medium cucumber
¼ teaspoon dill weed
⅛ teaspoon salt
½ cup dairy sour cream

Thinly slice unpared cucumber into bowl. Stir together dill weed, salt and sour cream; pour over cucumber slices and carefully mix.

*4 servings.*

### Market List

1 can (about 1 pound) fruit cocktail
1 bottle (7 ounces) carbonated lemon-lime
  beverage
  Horseradish
1 medium cucumber
  Lemon
  Dairy sour cream
1 package (10 ounces) frozen chopped
  spinach
1 package (1 pound) frozen French fried
  potatoes
2 packages (8 ounces each) frozen fish sticks
1 pint lemon or lime sherbet

# Ninety in the Shade

*When the temperature soars and your energy ebbs, play it kitchen-cool with a one-skillet main dish and crisp, chilly go-alongs. Corned beef, cabbage and hash brown potatoes cook happily together in a single utensil, making a dinner that saves you time, work and dishwashing. Cherry tomatoes and cheese-filled celery are colorful and cool accompaniments to the main dish. Even the delicious dessert, blended to the consistency of applesauce, is served icy cold. Alternate suggestion: If you're using an electric skillet, cook and serve the main dish at the table. You may even choose to serve it buffet-style on the patio so you can catch the passing breezes.*

---

*Corned Beef Hash Skillet
Cheese-stuffed Celery
and Cherry Tomatoes
Whole Wheat Rolls
Strawberry-Banana Frost
Milk     Coffee*

---

## TIMETABLE

**25 minutes before:**
  Shred cabbage

**20 minutes before:**
  Combine ingredients for main dish; start
    to cook
  Set table
  Make dessert and place in freezer
  Arrange celery and cherry tomatoes on
    dinner plates

**5 minutes before:**
  Add corned beef to hash browns; turn
    and heat through

Serve dinner.

## CORNED BEEF HASH SKILLET

  ½ small head cabbage
  3 tablespoons butter or margarine
  1 package (5.5 ounces) hash
    brown potatoes with onions
1¾ cups water
  1 teaspoon salt
  1 can (12 ounces) corned beef, cut up

With knife coarsely shred cabbage (3 cups). In large skillet, melt butter. Stir in cabbage, hash browns, water and salt. Cook uncovered over medium-high heat until liquid is absorbed and bottom is brown, 8 to 12 minutes.

Add corned beef; turn mixture with pancake turner and cook about 3 minutes longer or until meat is heated through.

*4 servings.*

## POTATO-EGG SCRAMBLE

*To vary the menu, substitute this recipe for Corned Beef Hash Skillet and adjust Timetable.*

    6 slices bacon
    1 package (5.5 ounces) hash
      brown potatoes with onions
    1 teaspoon salt
1¾ cups water
    4 eggs
    ¼ teaspoon salt
      Dash pepper

In large skillet, fry bacon until crisp; drain on paper towels. Pour off all but 3 to 4 tablespoons drippings from skillet. Add potatoes, 1 teaspoon salt and the water to skillet. Cook uncovered over medium heat until liquid is absorbed and bottom is golden brown; turn.

Beat eggs, ¼ teaspoon salt and the pepper; add to potatoes. Cook and stir until eggs are thickened throughout but still moist. Crumble bacon and stir into potato-egg mixture.

*4 to 6 servings.*

## CHEESE-STUFFED CELERY
## AND CHERRY TOMATOES

4 celery stalks
  About ¼ cup cheese spread
  Cherry tomatoes
4 parsley sprigs

Cut celery stalks diagonally in half. Fill celery pieces with cheese spread. On each dinner plate, arrange celery, tomatoes and parsley.

*4 servings.*

**Note:** Choose your favorite cheese spread for this recipe—Neufchâtel with pineapple, process cheese with bacon and process pimiento cheese spreads are all good.

## STRAWBERRY-BANANA FROST

1 package (16 ounces) frozen sliced
  strawberries
1 banana
  Softened vanilla ice cream

Cut frozen block of strawberries into 8 pieces. Peel banana and cut into 1-inch pieces. Place banana in blender container; blend until smooth. Add frozen strawberry pieces, one at a time; after each addition blend on high speed until smooth. Divide mixture among 4 dessert dishes and place in freezer until serving time. When ready to serve, top with ice cream.

*4 servings.*

**Note:** If you don't have a blender, partially thaw strawberries. Slice banana into dessert dishes and spoon strawberries over slices.

### Market List

1 can (12 ounces) corned beef
  Cheese spread
1 package (5.5 ounces) hash brown
  potatoes with onions
  Small head cabbage
  Celery
  Cherry tomatoes
  Parsley
1 banana
1 package (16 ounces) frozen sliced
  strawberries
  Vanilla ice cream

# Hasty-Tasty Steak Dinner

*Here's a nice variation on that most easily stored of freezer meats—cube steaks. Seasoned with salad dressing, dipped in flour and country-fried, they are equally appetizing summer or winter. Make this a help-yourself meal—pass steak and vegetables in serving dishes at the table. Bring the toaster to the table, too, and appoint a helper to make waffle fingers to order. One word of caution: When broiling sugar for Caramel Crunch, watch it closely. It cooks in less than two minutes.*

---

*Country-fried Minute Steaks*
*Succotash*
*Pickled Beets 'n Onion Rings*
*Parmesan Waffle Fingers*
*Caramel Crunch Sundaes*
*Milk     Coffee*

---

### TIMETABLE

**Ahead of time:**
  Chill pickled beets
  Make Caramel Crunch
**25 minutes before:**
  Set table
  Make salad; refrigerate
**15 minutes before:**
  Cook lima beans
  Coat steaks and panfry (using 2 skillets
    speeds up the browning)
**5 minutes before:**
  Add corn and butter to lima beans; heat
**Serve main course.**
**Prepare Caramel Crunch Sundaes and serve.**

## COUNTRY-FRIED MINUTE STEAKS

**2** tablespoons shortening
**4 or 8** frozen cube steaks (depending on size)
**½** cup bottled oil-and-vinegar salad dressing
**½** cup all-purpose flour

Melt shortening in 10-inch skillet. Dip steaks in dressing, then in flour, coating both sides. Panfry in hot shortening over medium-high heat, turning to brown both sides, about 4 minutes.

*4 servings.*

## SUCCOTASH

**1** package (10 ounces) frozen lima beans
**1** can (7 ounces) vacuum-pack whole kernel corn, drained
**1 to 2** tablespoons butter or margarine

Cook lima beans as directed on package. Drain. Add corn and butter to beans in pan. Heat through, stirring occasionally.

*4 servings.*

**Note:** If you prefer, substitute 2 packages (10 ounces each) frozen succotash for the frozen lima beans and corn; cook as directed.

## PICKLED BEETS 'N ONION RINGS

**Lettuce**
**1 jar (1 pound) pickled beets, chilled**
**½ medium onion**

Line serving bowl with lettuce. Drain beets thoroughly; place in bowl. Cut onion into thin slices; separate slices into rings. Arrange rings among beets. .

*4 servings.*

## PARMESAN WAFFLE FINGERS

Heat frozen waffles in toaster as directed on package. Spread with soft butter or margarine. Sprinkle with grated Parmesan cheese; cut into thirds and serve immediately.

### Market List

Four 4-ounce beef minute steaks or
8 frozen beef cube steaks
1 can (7 ounces) vacuum-pack whole kernel corn
1 jar (1 pound) pickled beets
Grated Parmesan cheese
1 onion
Frozen waffles
1 pint vanilla ice cream
1 package (10 ounces) frozen lima beans

## CARAMEL CRUNCH SUNDAES

**1 tablespoon soft butter**
**⅓ cup brown sugar (packed)**
**1 pint vanilla ice cream**

Spread butter on baking sheet, 15½x11 inches, leaving a 1½-inch border on all sides. Sprinkle sugar on buttered area.

Set oven control at broil and/or 550°. Broil sugar 3 to 4 inches from heat 1 to 2 minutes. (Watch closely—mixture burns quickly.) Crunch will have a lacy appearance. Allow to cool a few minutes on baking sheet. Remove with spatula and break into pieces.

Divide ice cream among 4 dessert dishes. Sprinkle broken crunch over ice cream.

*4 servings.*

**Note:** This quick topping is delicious on ice cream, custard, applesauce and other fruit desserts.

Remove crunch with spatula and break into pieces.

Sprinkle broken Caramel Crunch over ice cream.

25

# Meal that Holds Well

*Stew without stewing! Nothing could be simpler than this hearty, filling supper; it holds well for latecomers, too. The main dish is a delicious one-kettle combination of meat and vegetables spiked with chili powder, the dessert a bake-while-you-eat cobbler.*

Soup-bowl Stew
Lettuce Wedges
*with Cucumber Dressing*
Hard Crusty Rolls
Apricot Cobble-up
Milk     Coffee

### TIMETABLE

**Ahead of time:**
  Prepare meatballs; freeze
**20 minutes before:**
  Heat oven to 400°
  Combine ingredients for Soup-bowl
    Stew; heat to boiling
  Prepare cobble-up; place in oven
**10 minutes before:**
  Reduce heat for Soup-bowl Stew; cover
    and simmer
  Place rolls on ungreased baking sheet;
    heat in oven
  Set table
  Prepare salad
**Serve main course.**
**Remove cobble-up from oven and serve.**

## SOUP-BOWL STEW

1 recipe Make-ahead Meatballs (page 13)
1 can (1 pound) tomatoes
1 can (8 ounces) whole onions
1 can (8 ounces) whole potatoes
1 package (8 ounces) frozen mixed
  vegetables with onion sauce
1 to 2 teaspoons chili powder
1 cup water
1 beef bouillon cube or 2 teaspoons
  instant beef bouillon

In large kettle, combine frozen meatballs, tomatoes, onions (with liquid), potatoes (with liquid) and remaining ingredients. Heat to boiling, stirring occasionally. Reduce heat; cover and simmer 10 minutes.

*4 or 5 servings.*

## Timesaver

*No meatballs made? Substitute 2 cans (15¼ ounces each) meatballs in brown gravy; reduce water to ½ cup and omit beef bouillon.*

## LETTUCE WEDGES WITH CUCUMBER DRESSING

Chop ½ unpared medium cucumber. Place in bowl; stir in ½ cup dairy sour cream, ½ cup mayonnaise and 1 teaspoon salt. Serve over lettuce wedges.

*4 or 5 servings.*

Spread apricots and syrup evenly over batter in pan.

Serve Apricot Cobble-up warm with ice cream.

## APRICOT COBBLE-UP

    1  cup buttermilk baking mix
    ⅓  cup milk
    1  tablespoon brown sugar
    1  tablespoon soft butter or margarine
    ¼  teaspoon nutmeg
    1  can (1 pound 1 ounce) apricot halves

Heat oven to 400°. Mix all ingredients except apricot halves with fork to a soft dough. Spread in ungreased square pan, 8x8x2 inches. Pour apricots (with syrup) over batter. Bake 25 to 30 minutes. Serve warm and, if desired, with light cream or ice cream.

*4 or 5 servings.*

## Market List

2 cans (15¼ ounces each) meatballs in
   brown gravy (if you don't have Make-ahead
   Meatballs on hand)
1 can (1 pound) tomatoes
1 can (8 ounces) whole onions
1 can (8 ounces) whole potatoes
1 can (1 pound 1 ounce) apricot halves
   Hard dinner rolls
1 cucumber
   Dairy sour cream
1 package (8 ounces) frozen mixed
   vegetables with onion sauce

# Church at 11~ Dinner at 1

*Does your family like to sit down to a midday dinner on Sunday? Here's a menu they will welcome. The frozen turkey roast cooks in the oven while you're at church, comes to the table with the rest of the meal 20 minutes after your return. The cake is sliced frozen, thaws in 2 or 3 minutes under the broiler.*

---

*Orange-glazed Turkey Roast*
*Mashed Potatoes*
*Gravy*
*Brussels Sprouts and Carrots*
*Lettuce with Croutons*
*Toasted Honey-Banana Cake*
*Milk      Coffee*

---

### TIMETABLE

**Ahead of time:**
　Start roasting turkey—time will depend
　　on weight of roast and directions on
　　package
　Set table

**20 minutes before:**
　Transfer turkey to ovenproof platter and
　　glaze; continue roasting
　Drain carrots

**15 minutes before:**
　Start cooking Brussels sprouts
　Make salad

**10 minutes before:**
　Make gravy (if desired)

**5 minutes before:**
　Add carrots to Brussels sprouts; heat
　Prepare instant mashed potato puffs
　　as directed on package for 8 servings

**Serve main course.**

**Make dessert; serve.**

## ORANGE-GLAZED TURKEY ROAST

**2- to 3-pound frozen turkey roast**
**½ cup orange marmalade**
**Celery leaves or parsley**

Cook turkey roast as directed on package except—20 minutes before end of cooking time, remove roast to ovenproof platter. Spread orange marmalade over roast; place in oven and finish cooking. Garnish with celery leaves. If desired, make gravy as directed on turkey roast package. (For golden brown gravy, stir in a few drops of bottled brown bouquet sauce.)

*6 to 8 servings.*

**Note:** If package directions are not included with turkey roast, place roast on rack in open pan and cook in 325° oven until meat thermometer inserted in center of roast registers 170°.

### VARIATION
■ *Cranberry-glazed Turkey Roast:* Omit orange marmalade; heat 1 can (7 ounces) jellied cranberry sauce, ¼ cup corn syrup, 1 teaspoon grated lemon peel and 1 teaspoon lemon juice over low heat, stirring frequently, until blended.

29

## BRUSSELS SPROUTS AND CARROTS

**1 can (1 pound) sliced carrots**
**1 package (10 ounces) frozen Brussels**
   **sprouts**

Drain carrots, reserving liquid. Cook Brussels sprouts as directed on package except—substitute ½ cup reserved carrot liquid for the salted water; 5 minutes before end of cooking time, add carrots and continue cooking until Brussels sprouts are tender and carrots are heated through.

*6 to 8 servings.*

## LETTUCE WITH CROUTONS

 **1 small head lettuce, washed and chilled**
**½ cup bottled creamy onion salad**
   **dressing**
   **Herbed croutons**

Into bowl, tear lettuce into bite-size pieces (about 6 cups). Pour dressing over lettuce and toss. Divide salad among 6 to 8 salad bowls and sprinkle croutons over each.

*6 to 8 servings.*

### VARIATIONS
Omit the herbed croutons; sprinkle one of the following toppings over salads:

- Crumbled crisply fried bacon
- Chopped ripe olives
- French fried onion rings

## TOASTED HONEY-BANANA CAKE

**6 to 8 slices cut from frozen pound cake**
**2 bananas**
**¼ cup honey**

Set oven control at broil and/or 550°. Place cake slices on ungreased baking sheet. Cut bananas into ½-inch diagonal slices. Arrange slices on cake, completely covering top of each cake slice. Drizzle honey over banana slices. Broil 3 inches from heat 2 to 3 minutes or until honey is bubbly. If desired, serve with whipped topping, light cream or ice cream.

*6 to 8 servings.*

*Market List*

1 can (1 pound) sliced carrots
  Creamy onion salad dressing
  Honey
  Orange marmalade
  Herbed croutons
  Instant mashed potato puffs
2 bananas
1 package (10 ounces) frozen Brussels sprouts
  Frozen pound cake
2- to 3-pound frozen turkey roast

# Special for an Afternoon Out

*Your day to do volunteer work? Relax. A splendid pork roast, onion-flavored and wrapped in foil to insure juicy meat, can be slowly cooking while you're away. Home again, it's a quick quarter hour's work to cook vegetables, make gravy and warm dessert. Even your family will wonder how in the world you did it.*

---

*Pork Loin Roast*

*with Savory Gravy*

*Mashed Potatoes*

*Peas and Cauliflower*

*Caraway Rye Rolls*

*Dilled Cucumber Salad*

*Spiced Fruit Compote*

*Milk     Coffee*

---

## TIMETABLE

**3¾ hours before dinner:**
Put foil-wrapped roast in oven
Make salad; chill
Wrap rolls in aluminum foil
Set table

**15 minutes before:**
Heat Spiced Fruit Compote
Heat rolls in oven
Cook peas and cauliflower
Make gravy
Prepare instant mashed potato puffs
   as directed on package for 8 servings

**Just before serving:**
Mix salad

**Serve dinner.**

## PORK LOIN ROAST WITH SAVORY GRAVY

1 envelope (about 1½ ounces) onion
   soup mix
   5-pound pork loin roast
½ cup water
¼ cup all-purpose flour

Place 30x18-inch piece of heavy-duty aluminum foil in baking pan, 13x9x2 inches. Sprinkle soup mix in center of aluminum foil. Trim excess fat from roast. Place roast fat side down on soup mix. Fold foil over and seal securely, folding up ends of foil. Cook in 300° oven 3½ hours.

Open foil wrap; remove meat to warm platter and keep warm. Measure drippings and add enough water to measure 2 cups liquid. Pour into pan. Blend ½ cup water and the flour. Stir into liquid in pan. Heat to boiling, stirring constantly. Boil and stir 1 minute.

*6 to 8 servings.*

**Note:** If you have an automatic oven timer or programmed cooking system on your range, your roast can cook while you're away from home. Follow your range manual instructions. If roast is frozen, increase cooking time 10 to 15 minutes per pound. And keep in mind that pork roasts should be partially thawed before cooking begins—this insures even and thorough heat penetration.

## PEAS AND CAULIFLOWER

½ cup water
½ teaspoon salt
1 package (10 ounces) frozen cauliflower
1 package (10 ounces) frozen green peas
2 tablespoons butter or margarine

Measure water and salt into 2-quart saucepan. Place cauliflower in pan with peas on top. Cook as directed on package. Stir in butter.

*6 to 8 servings.*

## DILLED CUCUMBER SALAD

2 medium cucumbers
½ cup dairy sour cream
1 teaspoon sugar
½ teaspoon garlic salt
½ cup white wine vinegar or lemon juice
¼ teaspoon dill weed
  Lettuce
  Paprika or snipped parsley

Pare cucumbers and slice thinly into bowl. Stir together sour cream, sugar, garlic salt and vinegar; pour over cucumbers and toss lightly. Sprinkle mixture with dill weed. Cover and chill.

Just before serving, carefully mix and spoon into lettuce-lined bowl. Sprinkle with paprika or snipped parsley.

*6 to 8 servings.*

## SPICED FRUIT COMPOTE

2 cans (1 pound 1 ounce each) fruits for salad
¼ teaspoon cardamom
¼ teaspoon allspice

Heat fruits for salad (with syrup), cardamom and allspice to boiling. Serve warm.

*6 to 8 servings.*

## Market List

  5-pound pork loin roast
2 cans (1 pound 1 ounce each) fruits for salad
  Instant mashed potato puffs
  Cardamom
  Onion soup mix
  Caraway rye rolls
  Heavy-duty aluminum foil
2 medium cucumbers
  Dairy sour cream
1 package (10 ounces) frozen green peas
1 package (10 ounces) frozen cauliflower

# 30-Minute Dinners

*A traffic tie-up or a meeting that wouldn't end can leave you serene if you know how to cope. Armed with our market lists, you can shop on the way home and have one of these dinners ready in minutes.*

# Sit-by-the-Fire Supper

*For those chilly nights which lend themselves so well to a cozy supper in front of a glowing fire, here is the perfect meal. Steaming bowls of chicken and dumplings (made quickly from leftover cooked chicken) also contain vegetables. The two-green salad, with its gold and white sprinkling of chopped egg, is guaranteed to make a spinach-lover out of the most reluctant. The pie? It's given the homey touch of an orange marmalade glaze. Youngsters can eat from the coffee table, adults from end tables.*

---

*Quick Chicken 'n Dumplings*
*Pennsylvania Dutch Salad*
*Orange-glazed Apple Pie*
*Milk     Coffee*

---

### TIMETABLE

**Ahead of time:**
   Hard-cook eggs for salad
   Cut up chicken

**30 minutes before:**
   Put chicken and vegetables in kettle; heat to boiling
   Make dumplings

**20 minutes before:**
   Add dumplings to main dish; cook uncovered
   Set table
   Make orange topping for pie; set aside
   Make salad

**10 minutes before:**
   Cover chicken and dumplings; continue cooking
   Place pie in 350° oven

**Serve main course.**

**Heat orange topping; spoon over warm pie and serve.**

34

## QUICK CHICKEN 'N DUMPLINGS

*Pictured on preceding page.*

   2 to 3 cups cut-up cooked chicken or turkey
   1 can (1 pound) whole onions
   1 can (1 pound) sliced carrots
   1 can (1 pound) cut-up green beans
   1¼ cups chicken broth*
   1½ teaspoons barbecue spice
   ½ teaspoon salt
   ¼ teaspoon thyme
   Dumpling dough
   ¼ teaspoon dill weed

In 4½-quart kettle, combine chicken, onions (with liquid), carrots (with liquid), green beans (with liquid), chicken broth, barbecue spice, salt and thyme. Heat to boiling, stirring occasionally.

Mix Dumpling dough as directed on package of buttermilk baking mix except—before mixing ingredients, add dill weed. Drop dough by tablespoonfuls onto hot chicken and vegetables. Cook uncovered 10 minutes; cover and cook 10 minutes longer. (Liquid should just bubble gently.) Serve in soup bowls.

*5 or 6 servings.*

*Use canned chicken broth, or make chicken broth by dissolving 2 chicken bouillon cubes in 1¼ cups boiling water.

## TO COOK AND FREEZE CHICKEN

*Take advantage of free time and cook 1 or 2 chickens to use later in Quick Chicken 'n Dumplings or any other recipe calling for cut-up cooked chicken and/or chicken broth.*

Choose 3- to 3½-pound broiler-fryer chicken, cut up. Wash and place in kettle with giblets; add just enough water to cover. Add parsley, celery, onion, 2 teaspoons salt and ½ teaspoon pepper. Heat to boiling. Reduce heat; cover and simmer about 45 minutes or until thickest pieces are fork-tender.

Cool chicken in broth. Remove meat from bones and skin in pieces as large as possible. Cut up and pack tightly into pint freezer containers, with or without broth. Label and freeze. Storage time of chicken packed with broth is 6 months; without broth, 1 month.

*About 3 to 4 cups cut-up cooked chicken and 2 to 3½ cups broth.*

## PENNSYLVANIA DUTCH SALAD

 1 **small head lettuce, washed and**
   **chilled**
 5 **ounces spinach, washed and chilled**
 2 **hard-cooked eggs, coarsely chopped**
½ **cup chopped celery**
½ **cup bottled Italian salad dressing**

Just before serving, tear lettuce and spinach into bite-size pieces (about 6 cups) into bowl. Add eggs, celery and dressing; toss.

*5 or 6 servings.*

## ORANGE-GLAZED APPLE PIE

Heat commercially baked apple pie in 350° oven 10 minutes. Just before serving, heat ⅓ cup orange marmalade over medium heat. Stir in 2 tablespoons chopped walnuts. Spread over warm pie.

**VARIATIONS**

■ *Lemon-glazed Apple Pie:* Omit orange marmalade and walnuts. In small bowl, mix ½ cup confectioners' sugar, 1 teaspoon grated lemon peel and 1 tablespoon lemon juice until smooth.

■ *Crunchy Pecan-glazed Apple Pie:* Omit orange marmalade and walnuts. In small saucepan, combine ¼ cup brown sugar (packed), ⅓ cup chopped pecans and 2 tablespoons light cream. Cook over low heat, stirring constantly, until of glaze consistency, about 3 minutes.

*Market List*

1 can (1 pound) whole onions
1 can (1 pound) sliced carrots
1 can (1 pound) cut green beans
Orange marmalade
Barbecue spice
Walnuts
Celery
Fresh spinach
Commercially baked apple pie

# Supper in a Bun

*A good supply of delicious hamburger mix in the freezer can be tapped for an almost endless variety of hurry-up meals. Here we've coupled it with green beans and French fried onion rings and added decorative relishes.*

---

*Barbecue Green Bean Bunwiches*
*French Fried Onion Rings*
*Relish Kabobs*
*Jiffy Gel Sundaes*
*Milk      Coffee*

---

## TIMETABLE

**30 minutes before:**
Heat Barbecue Hamburger Mix with tomato juice
Heat oven to 425°
Set table

**25 minutes before:**
Cook green beans
Prepare Relish Kabobs; refrigerate

**15 minutes before:**
Place onion rings and buns in oven

**10 minutes before:**
Remove onion rings and buns from oven
Assemble bunwiches; return to oven
Measure gelatin into small bowl

**Serve main course.**

**Prepare Jiffy Gel Sundaes and serve.**

## BARBECUE GREEN BEAN BUNWICHES

1 pint frozen Barbecue Hamburger Mix (right)
⅔ cup tomato juice
1 package (9 ounces) frozen cut green beans
1 package (8 ounces) frozen French fried onion rings
4 large hamburger buns, split
8 lengthwise slices dill pickle
4 slices process American or mozzarella cheese
1 tomato, cut into 4 slices
Salad oil

Place container of frozen Barbecue Hamburger Mix in hot water just long enough to loosen sides. Combine mix and tomato juice in saucepan; heat over high heat 5 minutes. Reduce heat to medium; simmer uncovered 10 minutes or until heated through, breaking mix apart with fork and stirring occasionally.

Heat oven to 425°. While hamburger mix is heating, cook green beans as directed on package; drain. Arrange frozen onion rings and buns (cut side up) on ungreased baking sheet. Place in oven 5 minutes.

On bottom half of each bun, place about ½ cup hot hamburger mix and 2 pickle slices. Place a remaining bun half cut side up on each. Spoon ⅓ cup green beans on each and top with a cheese slice and tomato slice. Brush oil over tomato slices. Heat in oven with onion rings about 5 minutes.

*4 servings.*

36

# BARBECUE HAMBURGER MIX

*Make this ahead and keep in your freezer to use for menus on pages 36, 41 and 67 or for one of the variations below.*

**4 pounds ground beef**
**1 cup chopped onion**
**1 bottle (14 ounces) catsup**
**1 cup water**
**½ cup chopped celery**
**¼ cup lemon juice**
**2 tablespoons brown sugar**
**1 tablespoon salt**
**1 tablespoon Worcestershire sauce**
**½ teaspoon dry mustard**

Cook and stir ground beef and onion until meat is brown and onion is tender. Drain off fat. Add remaining ingredients. Cover; simmer 30 minutes. Cool. Divide mixture among five 1-pint freezer containers. Label each container, date and freeze.

To thaw frozen Barbecue Hamburger Mix, heat slowly in saucepan or thaw in refrigerator.

*Makes 5 pints.*

### VARIATIONS

■ *Barbecued Burger Buns:* Fill 6 to 8 buttered hamburger buns with 1 pint hot Barbecue Hamburger Mix.

■ *Baked Frank Rolls:* If desired, stir 1 cup shredded process American cheese (about 4 ounces) into 1 pint Barbecue Hamburger Mix. Split 8 to 10 frankfurter buns; remove part of bread from center of each. Spoon mixture into buns; wrap each in aluminum foil. Heat in 350° oven 30 to 35 minutes.

■ *Mock Pizza:* Split 6 to 8 hamburger buns; toast. Spoon 1 pint Barbecue Hamburger Mix over halves; sprinkle with shredded process American or mozzarella cheese and dash oregano. Set oven control at broil and/or 550°. Broil about 3 to 4 inches from heat just until cheese is bubbly.

Barbecue Green Bean Bunwiches

Relish Kabobs—so easy the children can make them.

## JIFFY GEL SUNDAES

⅓ cup boiling water
½ of 3-ounce package black
   cherry-flavored gelatin (3 tablespoons
   plus 1½ teaspoons)
1 pint vanilla ice cream or pineapple
   sherbet

Pour boiling water over gelatin in small bowl; stir until dissolved.

Scoop ice cream into 4 dessert dishes. Spoon hot gelatin mixture over ice cream.

*4 servings.*

**Note:** Keep remaining gelatin tightly covered in original container; to use, dissolve in 1 cup boiling water. Let set until firm.

## RELISH KABOBS

1 medium carrot
1 stalk celery
   Pitted ripe olives
1 large orange or grapefruit
   Celery leaves

With potato parer, cut carrot lengthwise into paper-thin strips. Roll up each strip and secure with wooden pick.

Cut stalk of celery into short narrow pieces; insert end of wooden pick in center of each. Place each olive on a wooden pick. Insert wooden picks with vegetables in orange; if necessary, cut thin slice from bottom of orange so it will stand upright. Place on serving plate on a "bed" of celery leaves.

*4 servings.*

## Timesaver

*Instead of making kabobs, cut carrot and celery into short, thin sticks. Arrange sticks and pitted ripe olives on serving plate.*

## Market List

Dill pickles
Tomato juice
1 package sliced process American or
   mozzarella cheese
1 package (3 ounces) black cherry-flavored
   gelatin
1 large orange or grapefruit
   Pitted ripe olives
   Celery
   Carrots
1 tomato
   Hamburger buns
1 package (9 ounces) frozen cut green beans
1 package (8 ounces) frozen French fried
   onion rings
1 pint vanilla ice cream

# Short-order Dinner

*Brighten up a rainy day with this colorful dinner. You'll applaud its convenience, especially at the end of a busy day. The meatballs and spinach come from the freezer. So do the shortcake rounds (unless you prefer the biscuit type). The rest of the meal comes right from the kitchen shelf, with the exception of the relishes. They chill in the refrigerator while you set the table and prepare the Meatballs Romanoff and spinach. Arrange the relish tray, and, for a surprise, try it with the cocktail sauce. From start to serving, this tasty nutritious meal takes just 30 minutes.*

---

*Meatballs Romanoff
Buttered Spinach
Relishes with Cocktail Sauce
Cherry Shortcakes
Milk        Coffee*

---

### TIMETABLE

**Ahead of time:**
  Prepare meatballs; freeze
**30 minutes before:**
  Prepare relishes; refrigerate
  Set table
**20 minutes before:**
  Prepare and cook Meatballs Romanoff
**15 minutes before:**
  Cook noodles
  Cook spinach
  Stir extract into pie filling
**Just before serving:**
  Drain noodles; stir in parsley flakes
    and butter
**Serve main course.**
**Prepare desserts and serve.**

## MEATBALLS ROMANOFF

  2 tablespoons butter or margarine
  1 tablespoon flour
  1 package (5.5 ounces)
    noodles Romanoff
1½ cups milk
  1 recipe Make-ahead Meatballs
    (page 13)
  2 teaspoons parsley flakes
  2 tablespoons butter or margarine

In large skillet, melt 2 tablespoons butter. Remove from heat; blend in flour and sauce mix. Gradually stir in milk. Heat to boiling, stirring constantly. Boil and stir 1 minute.

Add frozen meatballs. Heat to boiling. Reduce heat; cover and simmer 10 minutes. While meatballs simmer, cook noodles as directed on package. Stir parsley flakes and 2 tablespoons butter into noodles. Serve meatballs and sauce over noodles.

*4 to 6 servings.*

39

## BUTTERED SPINACH

2 packages (10 ounces each) frozen
  chopped spinach
2 tablespoons butter or margarine
  Vinegar

Cook spinach as directed on package. Add butter; toss until butter is melted. Serve with vinegar.

*4 to 6 servings.*

## RELISHES WITH COCKTAIL SAUCE

Arrange cauliflowerets, radishes and gherkins on serving plate or tray. Place small bowl of cocktail sauce for dip in center of plate.

## CHERRY SHORTCAKES

4 to 6 slices sponge or angel food cake
  or Warm Shortcake Rounds (right)
½ teaspoon almond extract
1 can (1 pound 5 ounces) cherry pie
  filling
4 to 6 tablespoons dairy sour cream,
  whipped topping, cottage cheese,
  yogurt or softened cream cheese
  Brown sugar

Place cake slices on dessert plates. Stir almond extract into pie filling. Spoon about ⅓ cup pie filling on each cake slice. Top each with 1 tablespoon sour cream and sprinkle with brown sugar.

*4 to 6 servings.*

## WARM SHORTCAKE ROUNDS

2⅓ cups buttermilk baking mix
 3 tablespoons sugar
 3 tablespoons butter, melted and
   cooled slightly
 ½ cup milk

Heat oven to 450°. Mix baking mix, sugar, butter and milk with fork to a soft dough. Spoon dough into 6 portions on ungreased baking sheet. With floured fingers, flatten and shape each portion into a round, ½ inch thick. Bake about 10 minutes or until golden brown.

*6 shortcakes.*

**Note:** Adjust Timetable if you're making the shortcake rounds.

Market List

1 can (1 pound 5 ounces) cherry pie filling
  Cocktail sauce
  Gherkins
1 package (5.5 ounces) noodles Romanoff
  Sponge cake
  Dairy sour cream
  Cauliflower
  Radishes
2 packages (10 ounces each) frozen spinach

# Shop on the Way Home

*Don't panic if you're late in getting out of the office and have a hungry family to be fed. Stop in at the store on your way home and pick up the makings for a hurry-up meal that combines two family favorites—chili and spaghetti. While the chili simmers, put the pot on to boil for the spaghetti, whisk the place mats into place and set the table. Let the children help with the salad. As soon as the spaghetti is done, you'll be ready to dish up this hot and hearty meal.*

*Chiligetti*
*Tossed Avocado Salad*
*Corn Chips*
*Orange Floats*
*Milk     Coffee*

## TIMETABLE

**Ahead of time:**
  Chill carbonated orange beverage
**30 minutes before:**
  Make chili mixture
  Set table
**15 minutes before:**
  Cook spaghetti
  Make salad
**Just before serving:**
  Put corn chips on table
  Drain spaghetti
**Serve main course.**
**Make floats and serve.**

## CHILIGETTI

1 pound ground beef
2 medium onions, chopped
  (about 1 cup)
1 can (1 pound) tomatoes
1 can (8 ounces) tomato sauce
1 tablespoon chili powder
1 teaspoon salt
1 can (15½ ounces) kidney beans
1 package (6 or 7 ounces) spaghetti
  (about 2 cups)

In large skillet or saucepan, cook and stir ground beef and onion until meat is brown and onion is tender. Stir in tomatoes, tomato sauce, chili powder, salt and beans (with liquid). Cook uncovered about 10 minutes or until of desired consistency.

Cook spaghetti as directed on package. Drain; turn spaghetti onto large platter and top with hot chili mixture.

*5 servings.*

### VARIATION
■ *Easy Chili:* Omit ground beef, onions, tomatoes and salt. Heat 1 pint frozen Barbecue Hamburger Mix (page 37), thawed, the tomato sauce or 1 cup tomato juice, the chili powder and beans 10 minutes or until of desired consistency.

41

## TOSSED AVOCADO SALAD

**1 small head lettuce, washed and chilled**
**1 ripe small avocado**
    **Bottled creamy Italian salad dressing**

Into bowl, tear lettuce into bite-size pieces (4 cups). Cut avocado lengthwise in half. Remove pit; peel and slice avocado crosswise into bowl. Pour salad dressing over lettuce and toss. Divide mixture among 5 individual salad bowls.

*5 servings.*

### VARIATIONS
Substitute one of the following vegetables or fruits for the avocado:

- ½ cup sliced zucchini
- 1 cup diced cucumber
- 1 cup uncooked cauliflowerets
- ½ cup sliced radishes
- 1 cup cooked vegetables such as green beans, lima beans, peas or mixed vegetables
- 1 unpared red apple, sliced
- 1 can (8½ ounces) grapefruit sections, drained, or 1 medium grapefruit, pared and sectioned

## ORANGE FLOATS

**1 quart orange sherbet**
**2 bottles (14 ounces each) chilled carbonated orange beverage**

In each of 5 tall glasses, place 2 scoops orange sherbet. Pour in orange beverage to fill glasses.

*5 servings.*

**Market List**

1 pound ground beef
1 can (1 pound) tomatoes
1 can (8 ounces) tomato sauce
1 can (15½ ounces) kidney beans
2 bottles (14 ounces each) carbonated orange beverage
    Corn chips
1 package (6 or 7 ounces) spaghetti
2 medium onions
1 small avocado
1 quart orange sherbet

# Emergency Shelf Special

*This production number pork loaf inlaid with mashed potatoes and frosted with golden cheese is too handsome to serve in the kitchen; it deserves to be platter-presented at the table. Once admired, it can be separated into meat and potato sandwiches and served one to a person. Adding a bit of fresh fruit to canned fruits for salad gives a touch of piquancy; the reserved fruit liquid is used in a sweet, slightly exotic sauce that adds interest to the dessert.*

> *Pork Supper Loaf*
> *Buttered Brussels Sprouts*
> *Combo Fruit Salad*
> *Cake Sundaes with Brown Sugar Sauce*
> *Milk    Coffee*

## TIMETABLE

**Ahead of time:**
  Bake cake
  Chill fruits for salad
**30 minutes before:**
  Heat oven to 400°
  Set table
**25 minutes before:**
  Make Pork Supper Loaf
**20 minutes before:**
  Start cooking Brussels sprouts
**10 minutes before:**
  Make salad
  Make sauce for dessert
**Serve main course.**
**Prepare dessert; serve.**

44

## PORK SUPPER LOAF

1 can (12 ounces) pork luncheon meat
Instant mashed potato puffs (enough for 4 servings)
1 cup shredded sharp Cheddar cheese (about 4 ounces)
1 tablespoon parsley flakes
¼ teaspoon garlic salt

Heat oven to 400°. Place loaf of luncheon meat wide side down on sizzle platter. Cut loaf into 8 equal slices. Place in oven to heat.

While meat heats, prepare potato puffs as directed on package for 4 servings except—omit salt; after fluffing potatoes with fork, stir in ½ cup of the cheese, the parsley flakes and garlic salt. Place ⅓ cup potato mixture between each 2 slices, keeping original loaf shape. Sprinkle remaining cheese over loaf. Bake about 5 minutes or until cheese melts.

Or, if desired, set oven control at broil and/or 550° and broil loaf 4 inches from heat about 5 minutes or until cheese melts and top is golden brown. Serve 2 slices meat with mashed potatoes between for each serving.

*4 servings.*

**Note:** If you don't have a sizzle platter, use 9x9x2- or 13x9x2-inch baking pan.

## BUTTERED BRUSSELS SPROUTS

1 package (10 ounces) frozen Brussels
  sprouts
¼ cup butter or margarine
1 tablespoon lemon juice

Cook Brussels sprouts as directed on package. Drain. Add butter and lemon juice. Heat over low heat until butter is melted. Toss sprouts in butter mixture until well coated.

*4 servings.*

**Note:** If your family especially likes Brussels sprouts, cook 2 packages; double the amounts of butter and lemon juice.

## COMBO FRUIT SALAD

1 can (1 pound 1 ounce) fruits for salad,
  chilled
1 banana or 1 large red apple
  Bottled sweet-and-sour salad dressing

Drain fruits for salad, reserving syrup°; place fruit in serving bowl. Slice banana into bowl; pour dressing over fruit and toss until fruit is well coated.

*4 servings.*

°*Use ¼ cup of the reserved syrup for dessert.*

**Note:** If desired, omit sweet-and-sour salad dressing; mix 2 tablespoons of the reserved syrup and ⅓ cup mayonnaise and pour over fruit.

## CAKE SUNDAES WITH BROWN SUGAR SAUCE

1 package (18.5 ounces) yellow or
  chocolate cake mix
1 pint vanilla ice cream
¼ cup reserved syrup from canned fruit
½ cup brown sugar (packed)

Bake cake mix in oblong pan, 13x9x2 inches, as directed on package. Cool. Cut four 2-inch squares from cake. (Freeze remaining cake or use as desired.)

Place cake squares on dessert plates; top each with scoop of ice cream. Heat reserved syrup and sugar, stirring occasionally, just until sugar is dissolved; spoon over ice cream.

*4 servings.*

Market List

1 can (12 ounces) pork luncheon meat
1 can (1 pound 1 ounce) fruits for salad
1 package (18.5 ounces) yellow or chocolate
  cake mix
  Instant mashed potato puffs
1 banana or apple
1 pint vanilla ice cream
4 ounces shredded sharp Cheddar cheese
1 package (10 ounces) frozen Brussels sprouts

# Steak House Dinner

*Most of us think of steak as a luxury, reserved for shoot-the-works celebrations—and so it is if we define steak as a T-bone or porterhouse. But steak needn't be a budget-buster if the definition is extended to include less expensive beef round or chuck, tenderized with a marinade. Add such traditional steak-house accompaniments as broccoli with hollandaise sauce and Parker House rolls. Follow with homemade chocolate sodas; the family will think they're dining out in style.*

---

*Broiled Round Steak or Thrifty Steak*
*Herbed Tomatoes*
*Broccoli with Hollandaise Sauce*
*Parker House Rolls*
*Chocolate Sodas*
*Milk     Coffee*

---

### TIMETABLE

**Ahead of time:**
　Chill club soda

**30 minutes before:**
　Marinate round steak (or prepare
　　Thrifty Steak for broiling)
　Set table
　Prepare tomatoes for broiling

**15 minutes before:**
　Broil round steak
　Cook broccoli
　Heat rolls

**About 10 minutes before:**
　If serving Thrifty Steak, broil

**About 5 minutes before:**
　Broil tomatoes
　Prepare hollandaise sauce

**Serve main course.**

**Make sodas and serve.**

## BROILED ROUND STEAK

　**1- to 1½-pound beef round or chuck**
　**steak, ¾ to 1 inch thick**
　**1 envelope (4/5 ounce) instant meat**
　**marinade**

Diagonally slash outer edge of fat on steak at 1-inch intervals to prevent curling (do not cut into lean). Marinate steak as directed on envelope of meat marinade.

Set oven control at broil and/or 550°. Broil steak 3 inches from heat about 7 to 8 minutes on each side for medium rare, longer for well done.

*4 or 5 servings.*

### VARIATIONS

■ *Broiled Round Steak with Mustard Butter:* Mix 2 tablespoons prepared mustard, 1 tablespoon snipped parsley, ¼ teaspoon onion salt and ¼ cup soft butter or margarine. Top hot steak with mixture.

■ *Broiled Round Steak with Sesame Butter:* Beat ¼ cup soft butter or margarine, 1 teaspoon Worcestershire sauce and ½ teaspoon garlic salt. Stir in 1 tablespoon toasted sesame seed. Top hot steak with mixture.

## THRIFTY STEAK

1 pound ground beef
1 tablespoon minced onion
½ cup milk
1 teaspoon salt
¼ teaspoon pepper
¼ cup dry bread crumbs

Mix all ingredients. Place in lightly greased shallow pan; pat mixture into shape of T-bone steak (1 inch thick).

Set oven control at broil and/or 550°. Broil meat 3 inches from heat 5 minutes. Turn, using 2 wide spatulas; broil 5 minutes longer for medium rare.

*4 or 5 servings.*

## HERBED TOMATOES

Remove stem ends from 4 or 5 medium tomatoes; cut each tomato in half. Set oven control at broil and/or 550°. Dot each half with ½ teaspoon butter or margarine. Sprinkle each half with salt, pepper and basil leaves, oregano leaves or savory. Broil tomato halves 3 inches from heat 5 minutes or until golden brown.

*4 or 5 servings.*

### VARIATIONS

■ *Cheese Broiled Tomatoes:* Omit butter and herbs; spread mayonnaise or French dressing on tomatoes and sprinkle with grated Parmesan cheese.

■ *Broiled Tomatoes with Onion:* Omit herbs; sprinkle chopped green onions or snipped chives over tomatoes.

47

## BROCCOLI WITH HOLLANDAISE SAUCE

**2 packages (10 ounces each) frozen broccoli spears**
**1 package (1¼ ounces) hollandaise sauce mix**

Cook broccoli spears as directed on package. Prepare hollandaise sauce as directed on package. Pour over hot broccoli.

*4 or 5 generous servings.*

## PARKER HOUSE ROLLS

Heat Parker House rolls in bun warmer or wrap rolls in aluminum foil and place in saucepan. Cover; place over low heat 10 to 15 minutes or until rolls are hot.

## Market List

1- to 1½-pound beef round or chuck steak, ¾ to 1 inch thick
1 package (1¼ ounces) hollandaise sauce mix
Chocolate syrup
Club soda
Instant meat marinade
Parker House rolls
4 or 5 medium tomatoes
2 packages (10 ounces each) frozen broccoli spears
Vanilla ice cream

## CHOCOLATE SODAS

For each soda, place 2 to 3 tablespoons chocolate syrup in tall glass. Fill glass ½ full with chilled club soda, ginger ale or carbonated lemon-lime beverage. Add 2 scoops vanilla ice cream, stirring after each addition. Fill glass with beverage. Serve soda with large marshmallow and red maraschino cherry on straw.

### VARIATION
■ *Chocolate-Peppermint Sodas:* Substitute peppermint ice cream for the vanilla ice cream.

# Lamb Chops by Popular Request

*Looking for a lamb dinner that's familiar but a bit different? Well, here it is! Potatoes and onions broil right along with the chops while carrots glaze in the skillet. Hesitant about the herbs? Use the family's favorite seasoning. Then top off the meal with one of these luscious desserts.*

---

*Herbed Lamb Chops*
*Broiled Potatoes and Onions*
*Honey-glazed Carrots*
*Quick Lettuce Slaw*
*Pears au Chocolat*
*or Apricot Sunny-side Up*
*Milk     Coffee*

---

### TIMETABLE

**Ahead of time:**
  Chill fruit and pudding
**30 minutes before:**
  Set table
  Prepare lamb chops
  Prepare potatoes and onions
**15 minutes before:**
  Broil lamb chops
  Prepare and heat carrots
  Shred head lettuce. Place on salad plates;
    top with favorite salad dressing and
    green pepper rings
**About 9 minutes before:**
  Turn lamb chops
  Add potatoes and onions to broiler rack
  Drain apricots
**5 minutes before:**
  Turn potatoes and onions; continue
    broiling
  Prepare dessert; refrigerate
**Serve dinner.**

## HERBED LAMB CHOPS

Select 4 shoulder lamb chops ¾ to 1 inch thick. Remove "fell," a paperlike covering, if it is on chops. Slash outer edge of fat on chops diagonally at 1-inch intervals to prevent curling.

Set oven control at broil and/or 550°. Place chops on rack in broiler pan. Sprinkle chops with ½ teaspoon rosemary, marjoram or oregano leaves. Broil chops 3 inches from heat about 6 minutes on each side or until brown. Season with salt and pepper. (Season after browning —salt tends to draw moisture to surface and delays browning.)

*4 servings.*

### VARIATIONS

■ *Garlic Lamb Chops:* Omit herbs; brush chops on each side with bottled oil-and-vinegar salad dressing and sprinkle with garlic salt before broiling.

■ *Curry Lamb Chops:* Omit herbs. Mix 2 tablespoons soft butter or margarine, 1 teaspoon parsley flakes and ⅛ teaspoon curry powder; brush chops on each side before broiling.

■ *Party Lamb Chops:* Omit herbs; after broiling chops on both sides until brown, place slice process Swiss cheese and onion slice on each chop. Broil about 2 minutes or until cheese melts.

## BROILED POTATOES AND ONIONS

Shape aluminum foil into a broiler pan, 10x7x1½ inches. Drain 1 can (1 pound) whole potatoes and 1 can (1 pound) whole onions. Place potatoes and onions in foil pan; dot with 1 or 2 tablespoons soft butter or margarine. Set oven control at broil and/or 550°. Place pan on rack in broiler pan. Broil 3 inches from heat 4 minutes. Turn potatoes and onions; sprinkle with seasoned salt and paprika; broil 3 minutes longer or until heated through.

*4 servings.*

## HONEY-GLAZED CARROTS

¼ cup honey
1 tablespoon butter or margarine
1 can (1 pound) whole carrots, drained

In medium skillet, heat honey and butter. Add carrots; simmer 10 minutes or until heated through, turning carrots to coat all sides.

*4 servings.*

## PEARS AU CHOCOLAT

1 can (1 pound) pear halves, drained
⅛ teaspoon mint extract
1 can (18 ounces) chocolate pudding

Place 2 pear halves in each of 4 serving dishes. Stir mint extract into pudding. Spoon pudding over pears. If desired, top each serving with frozen whipped topping.

*4 servings.*

## APRICOT SUNNY-SIDE UP

⅛ teaspoon almond extract, if desired
1 can (18 ounces) vanilla pudding
1 can (8¾ ounces) apricot halves, drained

Stir almond extract into pudding; divide among 4 dessert dishes. Top each serving with apricot halves, cut side down.

*4 servings.*

**VARIATION**

■ *Peach Sunny-side Up:* Omit almond extract and substitute 1 can (8¾ ounces) sliced peaches, drained, for apricot halves. If desired, top each serving with frozen whipped topping and sprinkle with mace.

Market List

4 shoulder lamb chops, ¾ to 1 inch thick
1 can (1 pound) whole potatoes
1 can (1 pound) whole onions
1 can (1 pound) whole carrots
1 can (1 pound) pear halves
1 can (18 ounces) chocolate pudding
Mint extract
Honey
1 green pepper

# Quick Trick Casserole Supper

*Here's a menu filled with quick tricks worth committing to memory for use whenever you're in a hurry. For instance, a salad made with chilled stewed tomatoes saves minutes of preparation—tomatoes are already seasoned. Separating frozen peas by running hot water over them in a colander makes them casserole-ready without thawing. A can of applesauce can be spiced up with cinnamon candies and warmed in the oven as cookies bake. Making cookies double-size saves time, too. All kinds of timesavers here!*

---

*Tuna Almondine with Peas*
*French Fried Onion Rings*
*Stewed Tomato Salad*
*Warm Spiced Applesauce*
*Jumbo Date Cookies*
*Milk     Coffee*

---

## TIMETABLE

**Ahead of time:**
  Chill tomatoes

**30 minutes before:**
  Heat oven to 400°
  Prepare and bake cookies

**20 minutes before:**
  Prepare and cook main dish

**15 minutes before:**
  Heat applesauce
  Heat 2 cans (3½ ounces each) French
    fried onion rings as directed on can
  Set table
  Prepare Stewed Tomato Salad

**About 2 minutes before:**
  Stir tuna into main dish; heat

**Serve dinner.**

## TUNA ALMONDINE WITH PEAS

1 package (6 ounces) noodles almondine
1 package (10 ounces) frozen green
  peas
2⅓ cups hot water
1 tablespoon butter or margarine
1 can (7 ounces) tuna, drained and
  broken apart

Combine noodles and seasoned sauce mix in 3-quart saucepan or large electric skillet. Place frozen peas in colander or sieve; run hot tap water over peas just until broken apart. Stir water into mixture in saucepan; add peas and butter.

Heat to boiling, stirring occasionally. Cover; cook over low heat (200 to 225° on electric skillet) 10 minutes. Stir in tuna; heat through, about 1 minute. Sprinkle almonds over top.

*4 or 5 servings.*

## STEWED TOMATO SALAD

**2 cans (1 pound each) stewed tomatoes, chilled**
**4 or 5 lettuce cups**

Drain tomatoes, reserving liquid to use as desired. At serving time, place a lettuce cup in each of 4 or 5 individual salad bowls. Spoon tomatoes into lettuce cups. If desired, serve with oil-and-vinegar dressing.

*4 or 5 servings.*

**Note:** 1 can (14½ ounces) sliced baby tomatoes or 1 can (1 pound) tomato wedges can be substituted for the stewed tomatoes.

## Timesaver

*Keep a few cans of stewed tomatoes on your cupboard shelf. Because they're already seasoned, they're a natural any time you want a quick salad.*

## WARM SPICED APPLESAUCE

**2 cups applesauce**
**2 tablespoons red cinnamon candies**

Heat oven to 400°. Measure applesauce and cinnamon candies into ungreased 1-quart casserole. Cover; heat 15 minutes. Stir; spoon into serving dishes.

If desired, heat applesauce and candies in saucepan over medium heat, stirring until candies are melted.

*4 or 5 servings.*

## JUMBO DATE COOKIES

**1 package (14 ounces) date bar mix**
**¼ cup hot water**
**1 egg**

Heat oven to 400°. Stir together date filling and hot water. Mix in crumbly mix and egg.

Drop dough by rounded tablespoonfuls about 2 inches apart on lightly greased baking sheet. Bake 8 to 12 minutes. Immediately remove cookies to wire rack.

*About 15 cookies.*

## Timesaver

*Mix makes these jiffy cookies; making them double size means they're double quick.*

### Market List

1 can (7 ounces) tuna
2 cans (3½ ounces each) French fried onion rings
2 cans (1 pound each) stewed tomatoes
1 can (about 1 pound) applesauce
  Red cinnamon candies
1 package (14 ounces) date bar mix
1 package (6 ounces) noodles almondine
1 package (10 ounces) frozen green peas

# Supper with a German Accent

*Traditional dishes of another country offer an easy way to get variety into your menu-planning. And although the originals may require long cooking, you can often cut preparation time to minutes with packaged foods. This hot potato salad, for example, uses scalloped potatoes. (No more burned fingers trying to slice potatoes before they cool!) Serve it with franks or bratwurst, add buttered cabbage and an easy version of red fruit pudding and your family sits down to a German-influenced meal that was prepared with American-style convenience.*

---

*Hot German Potato Salad
with Frankfurters
Buttered Cabbage
Cucumber Tomatoes
Pumpernickel Bread
Cherry Sparkle
Milk     Coffee*

---

### TIMETABLE

**30 minutes before:**
Hard-cook egg
Prepare and cook potatoes
Set table

**20 minutes before:**
Make sauce for dessert; keep warm
Divide cherries among serving dishes
Prepare and cook Buttered Cabbage
Prepare Cucumber Tomatoes; arrange
on dinner plates

**About 7 minutes before:**
Chop egg; add egg and vinegar to
potato mixture
Add frankfurters to the potatoes

**Serve dinner.**

## HOT GERMAN POTATO SALAD WITH FRANKFURTERS

1 package (5.5 ounces) scalloped potatoes
3 cups water
3 to 4 tablespoons vinegar
1 hard-cooked egg, chopped
1 pound frankfurters (about 10)

Combine potato slices and seasoned sauce mix in large skillet; stir in water. Heat to boiling. Reduce heat; cover and simmer 20 minutes, stirring occasionally.

Carefully stir in vinegar and egg. Arrange frankfurters on potatoes. Cover and simmer 5 minutes or until heated through.

*4 to 6 servings.*

### VARIATION
■ *Hot German Potato Salad with Bratwurst:* Substitute 1 or 2 packages (12 ounces each) bratwurst for the frankfurters. Before cooking potatoes, brown sausage in 3 tablespoons salad oil; drain on paper towels. Drain drippings from skillet.

Hot German Potato Salad with Bratwurst

## BUTTERED CABBAGE

**2-pound green cabbage**
**2 to 3 tablespoons soft butter or margarine**
**1 to 2 tablespoons lemon juice or wine vinegar, if desired**
**Salt and pepper**

Remove outside leaves of cabbage; wash cabbage and cut into wedges. Remove core and cut wedges crosswise into 1-inch slices. Heat 1 inch salted water (½ teaspoon salt for 1 cup water) to boiling. Add cabbage. Cover and heat to boiling. Cook 5 to 10 minutes or until just crisp-tender. Drain; stir in butter and lemon juice. Season with salt and pepper.

*4 to 6 servings.*

## CUCUMBER TOMATOES

**4 to 6 small tomatoes**
**2 medium cucumbers**
**2 tablespoons chopped onion**
**Bottled French dressing**

Cut each tomato into 6 sections, not cutting completely through. Pull sections apart slightly. Pare cucumbers and cut into ½-inch cubes. Mix cucumber pieces and onion; place an equal amount in each tomato. Top with dressing.

*4 to 6 servings.*

**Note:** If tomatoes are large, use a half for each serving. Cut each half into sections, not cutting completely through; spread sections like a fan and top with cucumber mixture and dressing.

## CHERRY SPARKLE

**1 can (1 pound) dark sweet cherries**
**2 teaspoons lemon juice**
**1 package (4¾ ounces) cherry-plum-flavored Danish dessert mix**

Drain cherries, reserving syrup. Measure syrup and lemon juice; add water to measure 2 cups liquid. Stir in dessert mix; heat to boiling. Boil and stir 1 minute. Divide cherries among 4 to 6 dessert dishes. Pour about ½ cup hot sauce over each serving. Serve warm.

*4 to 6 servings.*

**Note:** Leftover sauce can be stored covered in refrigerator. Serve as a pudding or heat and serve as a sauce over ice cream, cake or fruit.

Market List

1 pound frankfurters (about 10)
1 can (1 pound) dark sweet cherries
1 package (5.5 ounces) scalloped potatoes
1 package (4¾ ounces) cherry-plum-flavored Danish dessert mix
Pumpernickel bread
2-pound green cabbage
4 to 6 small tomatoes
2 medium cucumbers

# Serve It with Flair

*If your family has stopped commenting on your cooking and it's been weeks since anyone said "Gosh, that was good," maybe you've gotten into a rut. Why not serve a dinner that will make them sit up and take notice, a menu of foods that look and taste entirely different? Every dish in this dinner has a special twist. The canned ham is brilliantly topped by cherries flavored with crystallized ginger; the corn bread, rich with whole corn kernels; the tossed salad, studded with green beans and mushrooms; and the butterscotch parfaits, layered with cookie crumbs. All in all, we guarantee that this is a meal no one will ignore.*

---

*Baked Ham with Cherry Sauce*
*Green Bean-Mushroom Tossed Salad*
*Hot Double Corn Bread*
*Butterscotch Parfaits*
*Milk     Coffee*

---

### TIMETABLE

**Ahead of time:**
Chill beans and mushrooms

**30 minutes before:**
Heat oven to 400°
Heat cherry pie filling and ginger
Bake ham

**25 minutes before:**
Bake corn bread

**20 minutes before:**
Make parfaits; refrigerate
Set table

**10 minutes before:**
Make salad; serve on dinner plates

**Serve dinner.**

## BAKED HAM WITH CHERRY SAUCE

1 can (1 pound 5 ounces) cherry pie filling
1 to 2 teaspoons finely cut-up crystallized ginger
1 canned ham (1½ pounds)

Heat oven to 400°. In saucepan heat pie filling and ginger to boiling, stirring occasionally. Cut ham lengthwise into 4 to 6 slices; place slices in ungreased baking dish, 8x8x2 inches.

Spoon pie filling over ham. Bake uncovered 25 to 30 minutes. Serve ham slices topped with cherry-ginger mixture.

*4 to 6 servings.*

## GREEN BEAN–MUSHROOM TOSSED SALAD

1 can (1 pound) cut green beans, chilled
1 can (4 ounces) mushroom stems and pieces, chilled
½ small head lettuce, washed and chilled
2 teaspoons chopped pimiento
⅓ cup bottled Italian salad dressing
4 to 6 lettuce cups

Drain green beans and mushrooms. Into bowl, tear lettuce into bite-size pieces (about 2 cups). Add beans, mushrooms and pimiento. Pour salad dressing over vegetables; toss. Divide salad among lettuce cups.

*4 to 6 servings.*

## HOT DOUBLE CORN BREAD

1 package (14 ounces) corn muffin mix
1 can (1 pound) whole kernel corn, drained (reserve ⅔ cup liquid)

Heat oven to 400°. Grease baking pan, 13x9x2 inches. Prepare muffin mix as directed on package except—substitute the reserved corn liquid for the milk and stir in corn. Pour batter into prepared pan; bake 20 to 25 minutes.

*4 to 6 servings.*

## SESAME-CHEESE CORN BREAD

*Substitute this for the Hot Double Corn Bread if you like.*

Heat oven to 400°. Grease square pan, 8x8x2 or 9x9x2 inches. Prepare 1 package (14 ounces) corn muffin mix as directed except—stir in ½ teaspoon salt and 1 cup shredded sharp Cheddar cheese. Pour into prepared pan. Sprinkle batter with 3 tablespoons sesame seed. Bake 8-inch 20 to 25 minutes, 9-inch 15 to 20 minutes.

## BUTTERSCOTCH PARFAITS

1 can (18 ounces) butterscotch pudding
½ to ¾ cup graham cracker or cookie crumbs
Frozen whipped topping
4 to 6 maraschino cherries

In each parfait glass, spoon alternating layers of pudding, crumbs and topping. Top each with maraschino cherry. Refrigerate.

*4 to 6 servings.*

**VARIATIONS**

■ *Chocolate Crunch Parfaits:* Substitute 1 can (18 ounces) chocolate pudding for the butterscotch pudding and ¾ cup fruit-flavored corn puffs cereal for the crumbs.

■ *Lemon or Chocolate Parfaits:* Substitute 1 can (18 ounces) lemon or chocolate pudding for the butterscotch pudding.

Market List

1 can (1½ pounds) ham
1 can (1 pound 5 ounces) cherry pie filling
1 can (1 pound) cut green beans
1 can (4 ounces) mushroom stems and pieces
1 can (1 pound) whole kernel corn
  Maraschino cherries
1 jar (2 ounces) sliced pimiento
1 can (18 ounces) butterscotch pudding
1 package (14 ounces) corn muffin mix
  Crystallized ginger
  Graham crackers
  Frozen whipped topping

# Penny Pinchers, Good as Gold

*When it's the day before payday and the food allowance is depleted, or whenever nickels and dimes count, consider this savory dinner that tastes like a good deal more than it costs. The main dish, a stick-to-ribs combination of franks and corn with peppers in chili-spiked tomato sauce served over corkscrew macaroni, has the air of hearty Creole cooking about it. A few ripe olives dress up a simple lettuce salad and miniature marshmallows enrich the pudding cake. It's a made-in-minutes meal that's sure to please—all for pennies.*

---

*Hot Dog Creole
Corn Chips
Lettuce Wedges with Black Olives
Chocolate Marshmallow Pudding Cake
Milk     Coffee*

---

## TIMETABLE

**30 minutes before:**
Heat oven to 400°
Bake pudding cake

**20 minutes before:**
Prepare and cook Hot Dog Creole

**15 minutes before:**
Cook macaroni
Cut head lettuce into wedges; place on salad plates. Top with oil-and-vinegar salad dressing and garnish with black olives.
Set table
Put corn chips in serving dish

**Just before serving:**
Drain macaroni

**Serve main course.**

**Remove pudding cake from oven; serve.**

## HOT DOG CREOLE

8 frankfurters
1 tablespoon salad oil
1 can (15 ounces) tomato sauce
1 can (12 ounces) vacuum-pack whole kernel corn with peppers
½ to 1 teaspoon chili powder
½ teaspoon salt
2 teaspoons instant minced onion
1 package (5 ounces) corkscrew macaroni

Cut frankfurters into ½-inch pieces. Heat oil in large skillet. Add frankfurters; cook and stir until pieces are brown. Stir in tomato sauce, corn (with liquid), chili powder, salt and onion. Heat to boiling.

Reduce heat and simmer uncovered 10 minutes. While sauce simmers, cook macaroni as directed on package. Serve sauce over macaroni and, if desired, sprinkle with grated Parmesan cheese.

*4 or 5 servings.*

58

## SKILLET BEEF AND NOODLES

*To vary the menu, substitute this recipe for the Hot Dog Creole and adjust the Timetable.*

**1 pound ground beef**
**1 envelope (about 1½ ounces) onion**
  **soup mix**
**1 can (1 pound 12 ounces) tomatoes**
**4 ounces uncooked noodles**
  **(about 2 cups)**

In large skillet, cook and stir ground beef until brown. Stir in remaining ingredients; heat to boiling. Reduce heat; cover and simmer until noodles are tender, about 20 minutes, stirring occasionally.

*4 or 5 servings.*

## CHOCOLATE MARSHMALLOW PUDDING CAKE

Prepare 1 package (11 ounces) chocolate pudding cake mix as directed except—before baking, sprinkle 1 cup miniature marshmallows over batter in pan.

## CARAMEL COCONUT PUDDING CAKE

*Substitute this dessert occasionally for the Chocolate Marshmallow Pudding Cake.*

Prepare 1 package (11 ounces) caramel pudding cake mix as directed except—before baking, sprinkle ½ cup flaked coconut over batter in pan.

*Market List*

8 frankfurters
1 can (15 ounces) tomato sauce
1 can (12 ounces) vacuum-pack whole kernel corn with peppers
1 package (11 ounces) chocolate pudding cake mix
  Miniature marshmallows
1 package (5 ounces) corkscrew macaroni

# New Go-togethers

*An easy way to bring infinite variety to your day-in, day-out cooking is to put familiar foods together in new combinations. For example— both salmon and noodles Romanoff are probably familiar to almost everyone. But when they're combined they become a brand-new taste treat. You've undoubtedly cooked both peas and cabbage hundreds of times, but have you ever served them tossed together? Slices of orange make a bright garnish on any plate, but sprinkled with chives they become almost exotic. We've given you other variations on both of these. And with a little thought, we're sure you can dream up dozens of other new mix-mates of your own. Go ahead! Don't be afraid to experiment; it's fun to be original.*

*Salmon Romanoff*
*Buttered Peas and Cabbage*
*Chived Orange Slices*
*Warm Blueberry Cobbler*
*Milk     Coffee*

## TIMETABLE

**30 minutes before:**
Heat oven to 400°
Bake Blueberry Cobbler
Prepare and bake Salmon Romanoff

**15 minutes before:**
Set table
Shred cabbage
Cook peas
Prepare Chived Orange Slices; arrange on plates

**5 minutes before:**
Add cabbage to peas

**Serve dinner.**

## SALMON ROMANOFF

1 package (5.5 ounces) noodles Romanoff
1 can (7¾ ounces) salmon, drained and flaked
½ cup creamed cottage cheese

Heat oven to 400°. Prepare noodles Romanoff as directed on package except—increase milk to ⅔ cup and stir in salmon and cottage cheese. Pour into ungreased 1-quart casserole. Cover; bake 15 to 20 minutes.

*4 servings.*

**Note:** For 6 servings, use the 8.5-ounce package of noodles Romanoff. Use 1 cup milk, 1 can (1 pound) salmon and ¾ cup creamed cottage cheese. Pour into 1½-quart casserole and bake 20 to 25 minutes.

60

## BUTTERED PEAS AND CABBAGE

1 package (10 ounces) frozen
  green peas
1½ to 2 cups shredded cabbage
1 tablespoon butter or margarine
  Salt and pepper

Cook peas as directed on package except—
about 2 minutes before end of cooking time,
add cabbage. Simmer vegetables 1 to 2 minutes or until cabbage is just crisp-tender. Drain;
stir in butter and season with salt and pepper.

*4 servings.*

### VARIATION

■ *Buttered Peas and Lettuce:* Substitute 1½ to
2 cups lettuce chunks for the cabbage and simmer 1 to 2 minutes or just until lettuce begins
to wilt and look transparent.

## CHIVED ORANGE SLICES

4 oranges
1 teaspoon snipped chives

Pare oranges; cut each into 3 to 5 slices. Arrange slices on each of 4 dinner plates. Sprinkle about ¼ teaspoon chives on each serving.

*4 servings.*

### VARIATIONS

■ *Orange-Onion Slices:* Cut medium Bermuda
onion into very thin slices. Alternate orange
slices and onion slices on plates.

■ *Orange Ambrosia Slices:* Omit chives; sprinkle shredded coconut (plain or toasted) over
orange slices.

■ *Parsleyed Orange Slices:* Omit chives and
sprinkle snipped parsley over orange slices.

## WARM BLUEBERRY COBBLER

1 package (13.5 ounces) wild blueberry
  muffin mix
1 can (1 pound 5 ounces) blueberry
  pie filling
1 tablespoon lemon juice
1 teaspoon cinnamon

Heat oven to 400°. Drain blueberries from
muffin mix, reserving liquid. Stir together
reserved liquid, pie filling, lemon juice and
cinnamon; heat to boiling. Pour into ungreased
square pan, 9x9x2 inches, or baking dish,
11½x7½x1½ inches.

Prepare muffin mix as directed on package
except—spread batter evenly over hot pie filling mixture. Bake 25 to 30 minutes. If desired,
serve with cream or ice cream.

*6 to 8 servings.*

**Note:** To reheat leftover cobbler, cover pan
with aluminum foil and heat in 350° oven
about 10 minutes.

Market List

1 can (7¾ ounces) salmon
1 can (1 pound 5 ounces) blueberry pie filling
1 package (5.5 ounces) noodles Romanoff
1 package (13.5 ounces) wild blueberry muffin
  mix
  Chives
4 oranges
  Cabbage
  Creamed cottage cheese
1 package (10 ounces) frozen green peas

# Old Standby–
# Now a New Favorite

*Sometimes all you need to make a too-familiar food fresh and exciting is a new sauce. Take liver, for example. Here we've browned it as usual, then added it to a piquant onion and soy sauce for a new flavor. The pineapple-tomato salad adds color as well as a deliciously different taste sensation. Top the meal off with a dessert of brownie rounds and peppermint ice cream. Drizzle chocolate fudge sauce over the ice cream and the small fry will think it's a holiday.*

---

*Liver with Piquant Sauce*
*Creamed Peas and Potatoes*
*Pineapple-Tomato Vinaigrette*
*Peppermint Brownie Rounds*
*Milk     Coffee*

---

### TIMETABLE

**30 minutes before:**
   Heat oven to 350°
   Make salad; chill
   Bake brownies
   Set table

**15 minutes before:**
   Prepare liver and slice onion for
      main dish
   Cook peas and potatoes

**10 minutes before:**
   Brown liver and finish cooking main dish

**Serve main course.**

**Prepare dessert; serve.**

## LIVER WITH PIQUANT SAUCE

1 pound beef liver, sliced
¼ cup all-purpose flour
½ teaspoon garlic salt
¼ teaspoon paprika
⅛ teaspoon pepper
2 tablespoons shortening
   Piquant Sauce (below)

Cut liver into serving pieces. Place flour, garlic salt, paprika and pepper in plastic or paper bag. Shake liver in bag until well coated. Melt shortening in 10-inch skillet. Add liver and brown quickly on both sides, about 5 minutes. Remove meat to platter; keep warm while preparing Piquant Sauce. Add liver to sauce; heat through.

*4 servings.*

**PIQUANT SAUCE**

1 medium onion, sliced
1 tablespoon shortening
⅔ cup water
2 teaspoons cornstarch
2 teaspoons soy sauce

In same skillet, cook and stir onion in shortening until onion is crisp-tender, about 2 minutes. Blend remaining ingredients; pour into skillet. Cook, stirring constantly, until sauce thickens and boils. Boil and stir 1 minute.

## CREAMED PEAS AND POTATOES

1 can (15 ounces) sliced potatoes,
   drained
½ teaspoon savory, if desired
1 package (8 ounces) frozen green peas
   with cream sauce
   Salt and pepper

Add potatoes and savory to frozen green peas
in saucepan. Cook as directed on package.
Season with salt and pepper.

*4 servings.*

## PINEAPPLE-TOMATO VINAIGRETTE

   Lettuce
1 can (8½ ounces) sliced pineapple,
   drained
1 tomato
4 green pepper strips
   Bottled sweet-and-sour salad dressing

Arrange lettuce on each of 4 salad plates.
Place pineapple slice on each. Cut tomato
into 4 slices. Top each pineapple slice with
tomato slice and pepper strip. Chill. Serve
with salad dressing.

*4 servings.*

Cut brownies while warm into 4-inch circles.

Top rounds with ice cream and fudge sauce.

## PEPPERMINT BROWNIE ROUNDS

Heat oven to 350°. Prepare 1 package (15.5 ounces) fudge brownie mix as directed except—omit nuts and spread batter in greased jelly roll pan, 15½x10½x1 inch. Sprinkle ½ cup chopped walnuts or finely chopped salted nuts over batter and bake 15 to 20 minutes.

While warm, cut into four 4-inch circles. Top each circle with peppermint ice cream. If desired, drizzle chocolate fudge sauce over ice cream. Use remaining brownies as desired or cut into bars and freeze.

*4 servings.*

**Note:** An empty 1-pound 13-ounce can is the perfect size to cut 4-inch circles.

### Market List

1 pound sliced beef liver
1 can (15 ounces) sliced potatoes
1 can (8½ ounces) sliced pineapple
1 package (15.5 ounces) fudge brownie mix
Walnuts
1 tomato
1 green pepper
1 medium onion
1 package (8 ounces) frozen green peas with cream sauce
Peppermint ice cream

# Community Effort

*"Mom, can I help?"* This Potato Dog dinner offers something for even the smallest assistant to do. A youngster can spread mashed potato mixture on each frankfurter or man the toaster. Everyone makes his own dessert cookies at the table, sandwiching chocolate frosting between graham crackers. Tasty use-up suggestion: If there are leftover canned fruits in the refrigerator, add them to the ambrosia for extra flavor.

---

*Potato Dogs*
*Quickie Bean Salad*
*Buttered Toast*
*Banana Peach Ambrosia*
*Graham Cracker Cookies*
*Milk      Coffee*

---

## TIMETABLE

**Ahead of time:**
  Chill can of green beans
  (If you wish, make salad and allow to
    marinate)
**30 minutes before:**
  Make salad; refrigerate
  Prepare dessert; refrigerate
**20 minutes before:**
  Cut frankfurters; broil until heated
    through
  Prepare instant mashed potato puffs
    as directed on package for 4 servings;
    spread on frankfurters
  Set table
**About 8 minutes before:**
  Broil Potato Dogs
  Spoon salad into lettuce cups
**Serve dinner.**

## POTATO DOGS

1 pound frankfurters (about 10)
  Instant mashed potato puffs
  (enough for 4 servings)
½ teaspoon instant minced onion
1 tablespoon parsley flakes
1 teaspoon prepared mustard

Set oven control at broil and/or 550°. Cut frankfurters lengthwise, being careful not to cut completely through. Place cut side up on broiler rack. Broil 5 inches from heat 2 to 3 minutes just until heated through.

Prepare potato puffs as directed on package for 4 servings. Stir in onion, parsley flakes and mustard. Spread mixture over tops of frankfurters. Broil 5 inches from heat 5 to 8 minutes or until potatoes are brown.

*4 or 5 servings.*

**Note:** If you prefer, omit instant minced onion, parsley flakes and prepared mustard and stir in 1 tablespoon hot dog relish.

## QUICKIE BEAN SALAD

1 can (1 pound) cut green beans,
   drained
1 to 2 tablespoons chopped pimiento
   or sliced pimiento-stuffed olives
⅓ cup bottled Italian salad dressing
   Lettuce cups

Combine beans, pimiento and salad dressing; toss. Cover and refrigerate.

To serve, remove salad with slotted spoon and place in lettuce cups.

*4 or 5 servings.*

## BANANA PEACH AMBROSIA

1 large banana
1 can (1 pound) sliced peaches
   Flaked coconut

Diagonally slice banana into 4 or 5 serving dishes. Spoon sliced peaches (with small amount of syrup) over banana slices. Sprinkle each serving with flaked coconut.

*4 or 5 servings.*

### VARIATIONS
Substitute one of the following fruits for the sliced peaches:

- 1 can (13½ ounces) pineapple chunks
- 1 can (1 pound) fruit cocktail
- 1 can (1 pound 1 ounce) apricot halves
- 1 can (11 ounces) mandarin orange segments

## GRAHAM CRACKER COOKIES

For each cookie, spread canned chocolate frosting between two graham crackers.

Market List

1 pound frankfurters (about 10)
1 can (1 pound) cut green beans
1 can (1 pound) sliced peaches
1 can (16.5 ounces) chocolate frosting
1 jar (2 ounces) sliced pimiento
   Instant mashed potato puffs
   Flaked coconut
   Graham crackers
1 large banana

# After the Game

*This hearty, colorful 30-minute dinner will hit the spot with young appetites sharpened by an afternoon of touch football or stickball. The quick-cooked peppers are bright green and crisp, the meat and bean filling savory with tomato sauce. The pear salad can go right on the plate with the peppers to save cleanup time. And if there's any sundae topping left over, you could break it into bars and use as cookies.*

---

*Stuffed Peppers on the Half Shell*
*Pear Cheese Salad*
*Corn Bread Sticks*
*Praline Crunch Sundaes*
*Milk      Coffee*

---

### TIMETABLE

**30 minutes before:**
  Heat Barbecue Hamburger Mix
  Make Praline Crunch (or make ahead)
  Heat oven to 400°
  Bake corn bread
**15 minutes before:**
  Add beans and tomato sauce to Barbecue
    Hamburger Mix; continue heating
  Heat water for peppers; cut and wash
    peppers
**About 8 minutes before:**
  Cook peppers
  Set table
  Make salad
**Just before serving:**
  Cut corn bread into sticks
  Fill peppers
**Serve main course.**
**Make sundaes and serve.**

## STUFFED PEPPERS ON THE HALF SHELL

1 pint frozen Barbecue Hamburger Mix
  (page 37)
1 can (15½ ounces) red kidney beans,
  drained
1 can (8 ounces) tomato sauce
4 medium green peppers

Place container of frozen Barbecue Hamburger Mix in hot water just long enough to loosen sides. Place mix in 2-quart saucepan. Cover and heat over medium-low heat 15 minutes, stirring occasionally. Add beans and tomato sauce. Cover; cook over medium heat 15 minutes, stirring occasionally, or until heated through.

While mixture cooks, cut peppers lengthwise in half; remove seeds and membranes. Wash peppers; cook in boiling water about 5 minutes or until crisp-tender. Drain peppers; spoon an equal amount of meat mixture in each half.

*4 servings.*

## PEAR CHEESE SALAD

1 can (1 pound) pear halves, drained
Lettuce
1 to 2 tablespoons shredded Cheddar
cheese

Arrange pear halves on lettuce; top each with about 1 teaspoon cheese. If desired, serve with your favorite fruit salad dressing.

*4 servings.*

## CORN BREAD STICKS

1 package (14 ounces) corn muffin mix
1 egg
½ cup milk
½ teaspoon salt
1 teaspoon Worcestershire sauce
3 tablespoons sesame seed

Heat oven to 400°. Grease square pan, 9x9x2 inches. Measure contents of muffin mix; pour half (approximately 1½ cups) into mixing bowl. (Store remainder in package.)

Blend egg, milk, salt and Worcestershire sauce; stir into muffin mix until blended. (Batter will be slightly lumpy.)

Pour into prepared pan; sprinkle with sesame seed. Bake about 15 minutes or until golden brown. Cut in half, then cut each half into 8 sticks.

*16 sticks.*

## PRALINE CRUNCH SUNDAES

½ cup butter or margarine
⅔ cup brown sugar (packed)
4 cups of any of the following cereals:
Corn puffs
Fruit-flavored corn puffs
Fortified whole wheat flakes
Cornflakes
Whole wheat flakes
1 pint vanilla ice cream

Melt butter in large saucepan. Blend in brown sugar. Cook until thick and smooth, about 6 minutes, stirring constantly. Stir in cereal. Cook and stir a few minutes over low heat until cereal is coated. Spread in thin layer on ungreased baking sheet. Cool.

Divide ice cream among 4 dessert dishes. Crumble Praline Crunch; sprinkle 2 to 3 tablespoonfuls over each dish of ice cream. Store remaining crunch in airtight container.

*4 servings.*

### Market List

1 can (15½ ounces) red kidney beans
1 can (8 ounces) tomato sauce
1 can (1 pound) pear halves
1 package (14 ounces) corn muffin mix
Sesame seed
Corn puffs cereal
Shredded Cheddar cheese
4 medium green peppers
1 pint vanilla ice cream

# 35- to 45-Minute Dinners

*Short-order specialties can be as much fun to prepare as they are fast. And there's not a trace of menu monotony in any of these quickies. Here's how to make over a leftover, embellish a hamburger, serve foreign food with flair, surprise a bored dieter or showcase a brand-new dish.*

# Meanwhile, Back at the Ranch House

*Young buffs of the old West will take-kindly-ma'am to this cowboy collation calculated to delight the heart of any small boy. Let him invite a few of his "podners" for an afternoon of Wild West play. Then serve them a dinner that's right in the spirit of things: a casserole that looks like a wagon wheel, smoky green beans, Gold Rush Salad and Branded Brownies. You'll be the talk of the third grade, and the "best Mom of all" to your son.*

---

*Ham Chuck Wagon Special*
*Smoky Green Beans*
*Gold Rush Pear Salad*
*Branded Ice-cream Brownies*
*Cactus Juice      Coffee*

---

## TIMETABLE

**Ahead of time:**
   Chill pears
   Thaw cranberry-orange relish

**45 minutes before:**
   Bake brownies
   Initial ice-cream slices; freeze

**30 minutes before:**
   Prepare main dish
   Set table
   Arrange salad on salad plates;
      refrigerate

**10 minutes before:**
   Heat beans

**About 6 minutes before:**
   Arrange meat strips on casserole and heat
      in oven
   For Cactus Juice, stir 2 drops yellow food
      color into each 8-ounce glass of milk

**Serve dinner.**

## HAM CHUCK WAGON SPECIAL
*Pictured on preceding page.*

Cut 8 strips, each 3½x½x½ inch, from 1 pound cooked ham or 1 can (12 ounces) pork luncheon meat; cut remaining meat into cubes.

Prepare 1 package (8 ounces) macaroni and Cheddar dinner as directed for saucepan method except—stir in cubed meat and ¼ cup chopped green pepper with the sauce mix. Pour into ungreased 1½-quart casserole and arrange meat strips in spoke design on top.

Heat uncovered in 350° oven 5 minutes or until strips are heated through.

*4 or 5 servings.*

### VARIATIONS
■ *Frankfurter Chuck Wagon Special:* Omit ham; stir in 6 frankfurters, sliced.

■ *Tuna Chuck Wagon Special:* Omit ham; stir in 1 can (7 ounces) tuna, drained and flaked.

■ *Chicken Chuck Wagon Special:* Omit ham; stir in 1 to 1½ cups cut-up cooked chicken or turkey.

## SMOKY GREEN BEANS

2 cans (1 pound each) whole green
  beans*
½ teaspoon hickory-smoked salt,
  if desired
2 tablespoons butter or margarine

Heat green beans. Drain; add salt and butter. Heat until butter is melted, stirring beans occasionally.

*4 or 5 generous servings.*

*°You can substitute 2 packages (9 ounces each) frozen cut green beans for the whole green beans; cook as directed on package.*

**Note:** To delight the heart of a small boy, place a strip of pimiento around each serving for a "lasso."

## GOLD RUSH PEAR SALAD

1 can (1 pound) pear halves,
  chilled and drained
  Lettuce
1 package (10 ounces) frozen cranberry-
  orange relish, thawed

Place pear halves cut side up on lettuce. Fill cavity of each pear with cranberry-orange relish.

*4 or 5 servings.*

**Note:** For a salad especially appealing to children, omit cranberry-orange relish; fill cavity of each pear with spoonful each peanut butter and red jelly.

### VARIATION
■ *Golden Ring Salad:* Substitute slices of pineapple for pear halves and, if desired, garnish salads with snipped fresh mint.

## BRANDED ICE-CREAM BROWNIES

Bake 1 package (15.5 ounces) fudge brownie mix as directed. Cool. Cut 1-pint brick vanilla ice cream into 4 or 5 slices. Place slices on tray or baking sheet. Snip corner of 1 envelope (1 ounce) premelted unsweetened chocolate; form initials of each guest on an ice-cream slice. Freeze until initials are set. Or, if desired, outline initials on ice-cream slices with semisweet chocolate pieces.

Cut brownies into 3-inch squares. Top 4 or 5 brownie squares with ice-cream slices.

*4 or 5 servings.*

# East Meets West

With a little Oriental cunning on your part, Sunday's roast can make a Tuesday night appearance so artfully disguised that no one will guess its origin. Just cut cooked pork, chicken or turkey into cubes and mix with such canned delicacies as bean sprouts and mushrooms. Serve on Chinese-style noodles and you have a perfect chow mein. Add generous portions of rice sparked with chives, a citrus fruit salad served with sweet and sour dressing, and finish off with all-American gingerbread topped with candy-laced whipped cream. Leftovers? It's a meal fit for a king!

---

*Pork Chow Mein*
*White Rice with Chives*
*or Browned Rice*
*Grapefruit-Orange Salad*
*Gingerbread with Toffee Crunch Topping*
*Milk     Coffee*

---

## TIMETABLE

**Ahead of time:**
   Cut up pork roast

**45 minutes before:**
   Heat oven to 350°
   Chill fruits for salad
   Bake gingerbread
   Cut up vegetables for chow mein

**30 minutes before:**
   Cook Pork Chow Mein
   Make topping for gingerbread;
      refrigerate
   Set table

**15 minutes before:**
   Cook rice; keep hot
   Make salad

**Serve dinner.**

## PORK CHOW MEIN

2 to 3 cups cubed cooked pork roast
1 medium onion, sliced
2 cups diagonally sliced celery
3 tablespoons salad oil
1 can (6 ounces) sliced mushrooms
1 can (1 pound) bean sprouts, drained
2 tablespoons chopped pimiento
1 can (10½ ounces) condensed chicken broth (1¼ cups)
¼ cup soy sauce
3 tablespoons cornstarch
2 cans (3 ounces each) chow mein noodles

In large skillet, cook and stir pork, onion and celery in oil until onion is tender. Stir in mushrooms (with liquid), bean sprouts, pimiento and chicken broth. Blend soy sauce and cornstarch; stir into vegetable mixture. Cook, stirring constantly, until mixture thickens and boils. Boil and stir 1 minute. Serve over chow mein noodles.

*4 to 6 servings.*

### VARIATION
■ *Chicken or Turkey Chow Mein:* Substitute 2 to 3 cups cut-up cooked chicken or turkey for the pork.

72

## WHITE RICE WITH CHIVES

Prepare instant rice as directed on package for 4 or 6 servings. Stir 1 tablespoon snipped chives into hot rice. Serve with soy sauce.

## BROWNED RICE

Prepare instant rice as directed on package for 4 or 6 servings except—before adding water and salt, cook and stir rice in 3 tablespoons melted butter or margarine over medium-high heat until golden brown, about 5 minutes. If desired, stir 1 tablespoon snipped chives into hot cooked rice.

## Timesaver

*Prepare 2 packages (12 ounces each) frozen buttered rice as directed on package. Start with hot tap water for the frozen pouches, and you'll shave preparation time even further.*

## GRAPEFRUIT-ORANGE SALAD

1 can (1 pound) grapefruit sections, drained
1 can (11 ounces) mandarin orange segments, drained
Lettuce
Sweet-and-sour salad dressing

Arrange grapefruit sections and orange segments on lettuce. Drizzle about 1 teaspoon salad dressing over each serving.

*4 to 6 servings.*

## QUICK ORANGE-PINEAPPLE GEL

*This salad can be substituted for Grapefruit-Orange Salad. Adjust the Timetable by making the salad first and placing it in the freezer 30 minutes while preparing the meal.*

Drain 1 can (11 ounces) mandarin orange segments and pineapple tidbits, reserving syrup. Add enough water to reserved syrup to measure 1 cup liquid. Heat liquid to boiling.

Empty 1 package (3 ounces) orange-pineapple-flavored gelatin into bowl. Pour liquid over gelatin, stirring until gelatin is dissolved. Add 7 to 10 ice cubes; stir until thickened. Remove any ice cubes that remain; stir in orange segments and pineapple tidbits. Chill until set.

*4 to 6 servings.*

## Timesaver

*The ice cubes help the gelatin to set more quickly; remember this shortcut method whenever you want a gelatin salad or dessert in a hurry.*

## GINGERBREAD WITH TOFFEE CRUNCH TOPPING

Bake 1 package (14.5 ounces) gingerbread mix as directed. Cut into squares and serve warm, topped with Toffee Crunch Topping (below).

Toffee Crunch Topping: Crush 1 bar (¾ ounce) chocolate-coated toffee candy; fold into 1 cup frozen whipped topping or whipped cream.

### VARIATIONS
Omit candy bar; fold in one of the following:

- ½ cup chopped salted peanuts
- ¼ cup flaked coconut
- ¼ cup crushed peanut brittle
- ¼ cup crushed peppermint stick candy
- 2 tablespoons brown sugar

73

# Easy on the Cook

*Motto for a well-organized lady of the house: Make it ahead! A little preplanning is all it takes and, once it becomes a habit, it's like having a helper in the kitchen. Here, the Lasagne can be made the night before and stored in the refrigerator. At dinner time, it's popped into the oven to bake while you make the breadsticks and toss the salad. What a surprised family you'll have when they see the delicious meal you produced while you sat down with the paper!*

> Lasagne
> Zucchini Salad
> Garlic Breadsticks
> Sunny Fruit Trio
> Milk     Coffee

## TIMETABLE

**Several hours ahead of time:**
Make Lasagne; refrigerate

**40 minutes before:**
Heat oven to 350°
Put Lasagne in oven
Drain and chill peaches
Set table
Prepare breadsticks for baking

**15 minutes before:**
Put breadsticks in oven
Remove orange concentrate from freezer
Make salad

**Just before serving:**
Sprinkle Lasagne with Parmesan cheese

**Serve main course.**

**Make and serve dessert.**

74

## LASAGNE

1 pound ground beef
3 cans (8 ounces each) tomato sauce
  or 1 can (6 ounces) tomato paste
  plus 1 can (1 pound) whole tomatoes
½ teaspoon salt
¼ teaspoon pepper
½ teaspoon oregano leaves
1 package (8 ounces) lasagne noodles
1 package (8 ounces) shredded or
  sliced Swiss or mozzarella cheese
1½ cups (12-ounce carton) creamed
  cottage cheese
⅓ cup grated Parmesan cheese

In medium skillet, cook and stir ground beef until brown. Drain off fat. Stir in tomato sauce, salt, pepper and oregano. Heat to boiling, stirring occasionally. Reduce heat; cover and simmer 20 minutes.

Cook noodles as directed on package. Drain. In ungreased baking dish, 11½x7½x1½ inches, alternate layers of one third each noodles, Swiss cheese, cottage cheese and meat sauce, ending with 1¼ cups meat sauce. (At this point, casserole can be covered and refrigerated several hours before baking.)

Heat oven to 350°. Bake casserole uncovered 40 minutes. Sprinkle with Parmesan cheese.

*6 servings.*

## ZUCCHINI SALAD

1 small head lettuce,
   washed and chilled
2 small zucchini
½ cup bottled Italian salad dressing
1 can (3½ ounces) French fried onion
   rings

Into salad bowl, tear lettuce into bite-size pieces (about 4 cups). Wash zucchini; remove stem and blossom ends. Cut crosswise diagonally into thin slices; add to lettuce. If desired, 1 can (4 ounces) mushroom stems and pieces, drained, can be added. Pour salad dressing over vegetables; toss. Arrange onion rings over salad.

*6 servings.*

### VARIATIONS

■ *Gold and Green Salad:* Substitute 1 cup cooked green peas, ¼ cup cauliflowerets and 2 carrots, sliced, for the zucchini.

■ *Tossed Radish Salad:* Substitute 1 cup sliced radishes for the zucchini and add 3 green onions, sliced (about 2 tablespoons).

## GARLIC BREADSTICKS

Heat oven to 350°. Spread 4 to 6 slices white bread with soft butter or margarine and sprinkle with garlic salt. Cut each slice into 4 sticks; place on ungreased baking sheet. Heat in oven until crisp and golden brown, about 15 minutes.

## SUNNY FRUIT TRIO

2 small bananas
1 can (1 pound 13 ounces) sliced
   peaches, drained and chilled
6 tablespoons thawed orange juice
   concentrate

Peel bananas; cut bananas into ½-inch slices, dividing slices equally among 6 dessert dishes. Spoon peaches over banana slices and top each serving with 1 tablespoon orange juice concentrate. If desired, garnish each with maraschino cherry or sprig of mint.

*6 servings.*

## RIVIERA PEACHES

*Substitute this dessert occasionally for Sunny Fruit Trio.*

6 peach halves
1 package (10 ounces) frozen raspberries,
   thawed
1 pint vanilla ice cream

Place a peach half in each of 6 dessert dishes. Spoon raspberries over peaches and top each serving with a scoop of ice cream.

*6 servings.*

# One to a Customer

*When minutes count, instead of baking a full-size meat loaf, try individual mini loaves that cook in half the time. Top them with canned Spanish rice and tomato sauce and wind up the meal with Butterscotch Frosties (frozen pudding on sticks) served bouquet-style in a glass flower holder.*

---

*Mini Meat Loaves*
*with Spanish Rice*
*Italian Green Beans with Mushrooms*
*Toasted French Bread*
*Butterscotch Frosties or Butterscotch Whip*
*Milk     Coffee*

---

## TIMETABLE

**Ahead of time:**
   Prepare Butterscotch Frosties; freeze
**40 minutes before:**
   Heat oven to 425°
   Prepare meat loaves
**30 minutes before:**
   Place meat loaves in oven
   If serving Butterscotch Whip, prepare
      and refrigerate
   Set table
   Prepare bread for heating
**15 minutes before:**
   Cook green beans
   Spoon topping on meat loaves
**5 minutes before:**
   Heat bread
   Add mushrooms to beans; heat
**Serve dinner.**

## MINI MEAT LOAVES WITH SPANISH RICE

1½ **pounds ground beef**
¼ **cup instant minced onion**
¾ **cup dry bread crumbs**
1½ **teaspoons salt**
 1 **teaspoon parsley flakes**
¼ **teaspoon pepper**
 1 **teaspoon Worcestershire sauce**
 1 **egg**
⅓ **cup milk**
 1 **can (15 ounces) Spanish rice**
 1 **can (8 ounces) tomato sauce**

Heat oven to 425°. Mix thoroughly all ingredients except Spanish rice and tomato sauce. Shape meat mixture into 6 small loaves, each 4x2½ inches. Place in ungreased square pan, 9x9x2 inches. Bake 15 minutes. Top each loaf with about ⅓ cup Spanish rice; spoon tomato sauce over rice. Bake 10 minutes longer or until meat is done and rice is heated through.

*4 to 6 servings.*

### VARIATIONS
Omit Spanish rice and tomato sauce and top loaves with one of the following:

■ 1 can (10¾ ounces) condensed Cheddar cheese soup

■ 1 can (10¾ ounces) condensed tomato soup

■ *Mini Meat Loaves Italiano:* Substitute 1 can (15¼ ounces) spaghetti in tomato sauce or 1 can (15½ ounces) ravioli for the Spanish rice.

## ITALIAN GREEN BEANS WITH MUSHROOMS

2 packages (9 ounces each) frozen Italian
  green beans
1 can (4 ounces) mushroom stems
  and pieces
1 tablespoon butter or margarine

Cook Italian green beans as directed on package except—during last few minutes of cooking, add mushrooms (with liquid) to heat through. Drain; stir in butter.

*4 to 6 servings.*

## TOASTED FRENCH BREAD

Heat oven to 425°. Cut half of 1-pound loaf French bread diagonally into 1-inch slices. Spread cut surfaces with ¼ cup soft butter or margarine; sprinkle with garlic salt. Reassemble half loaf; wrap in aluminum foil and heat in oven 5 minutes.

*4 to 6 servings.*

## BUTTERSCOTCH FROSTIES

1 can (18 ounces) butterscotch pudding
¼ cup milk
3 teaspoons multicolored nonpareils

Blend pudding and milk. Place six 4-ounce paper cups in muffin cups and sprinkle ½ teaspoon multicolored nonpareils in each. Divide pudding mixture equally among cups. Insert ice-cream stick in center of each; freeze until firm, about 4 hours. Let stand at room temperature 5 minutes before removing paper cups.

*6 frosties.*

### VARIATION
■ *Chocolate Frosties:* Substitute 1 can (18 ounces) chocolate pudding for the butterscotch.

## BUTTERSCOTCH WHIP

1 envelope (about 2 ounces) dessert
  topping mix
1 can (18 ounces) butterscotch pudding

Prepare dessert topping mix as directed on package. Fold in pudding. Divide mixture equally among 6 dessert dishes; refrigerate.

*6 servings.*

### VARIATION
■ *Chocolate Whip:* Substitute 1 can (18 ounces) chocolate pudding for the butterscotch.

## FRUIT MEDLEY SALAD

*Serve this fruit dessert occasionally as a change of pace in the menu.*

1 can (8 ounces) fruit cocktail, drained
2 bananas, peeled and sliced crosswise
1 small apple, cut into small pieces
½ cup halved seedless green grapes
5 maraschino cherries, cut up
¼ cup miniature marshmallows
½ cup chilled whipping cream

Combine fruit cocktail, bananas, apple, grapes, cherries and marshmallows in bowl. In chilled bowl, beat cream until stiff. Fold fruit into whipped cream.

*4 to 6 servings.*

# Steak with Style

*Looking for a quick special-occasion dinner? Here's a colorful combination of food with an Oriental flavor that takes just 45 minutes to prepare. The steak is cut into strips and simmered in a rich sauce, the Mandarin Salad has an exotic honey-spiked dressing. You won't be sorry you tried this one!*

---

*Pepper Steak*
*Fluffy Rice*
*Mandarin Salad     Sesame Rolls*
*Pineapple Sherbet*
*Almond Butter Cookies*
*Milk     Tea*

---

## TIMETABLE

**Ahead of time:**
Bake Almond Butter Cookies

**45 minutes before:**
Make salad; chill
Cut meat into strips and brown

**30 minutes before:**
Add water, onion, garlic salt and ginger
to meat; begin to simmer
Set table

**15 minutes before:**
Add green pepper strips to meat mixture
Arrange salad on plates

**10 minutes before:**
Heat rolls
Cook instant rice
Blend cornstarch mixture and stir into
meat mixture

**About 3 minutes before:**
Place tomatoes on meat mixture; heat
through

**Serve main course.**
Divide sherbet among dishes; serve dessert.

## PEPPER STEAK

*Pictured on cover.*

1½ **pounds top beef round or**
**sirloin steak, about 1 inch thick**
¼ **cup salad oil**
1 **cup water**
1 **medium onion, cut into ¼-inch slices**
½ **teaspoon garlic salt**
¼ **teaspoon ginger**
2 **medium green peppers, cut into**
**strips (¾ inch wide)**
**Instant rice**
1 **tablespoon cornstarch**
2 **to 3 teaspoons sugar, if desired**
2 **tablespoons soy sauce**
2 **medium tomatoes**

Trim fat from meat; cut meat into strips, 2x1x¼ inch. Heat oil in large skillet. Add meat; cook, turning frequently, until brown, about 5 minutes. Stir in water, onion, garlic salt and ginger. Heat to boiling; reduce heat. Cover and simmer 12 to 15 minutes for round steak, 5 to 8 minutes for sirloin. Add green pepper strips during last 5 minutes of simmering. While meat simmers, cook instant rice as directed on package for 4 or 6 servings.

Blend cornstarch, sugar and soy sauce; stir into meat mixture. Cook, stirring constantly, until mixture thickens and boils. Boil and stir 1 minute. Cut each tomato into eighths and place on meat mixture. Cover; cook over low heat just until tomatoes are heated through, about 3 minutes. Serve with rice.

*4 or 5 servings.*

It's easy to cut meat that's been partially frozen.

Cut onion, pepper and tomatoes while meat simmers.

## MANDARIN SALAD

1 small apple
1 can (8¼ ounces) seedless grapes, drained, or 1 cup fresh seedless green grapes
1 can (11 ounces) mandarin orange segments, drained
2 tablespoons honey
¼ teaspoon cinnamon
2 tablespoons lemon juice
Lettuce

Quarter unpared apple and slice thinly into bowl. Add grapes and orange segments. Blend honey, cinnamon and lemon juice; pour over fruit. Cover and chill. At serving time, toss fruit until well coated; serve on lettuce.

*4 or 5 servings.*

### VARIATIONS

Substitute one of the following fruit combinations for the apple, grapes and orange segments:

■ Honeydew melon slices and balls of cantaloupe and watermelon

■ Orange and grapefruit sections and avocado slices

■ Banana pieces (dipped in pineapple syrup and rolled in chopped peanuts) and pineapple spears

## SESAME ROLLS

Heat sesame rolls in bun warmer or wrap rolls in aluminum foil and place in saucepan. Cover; place over low heat 10 to 15 minutes or until rolls are hot.

Flatten cookies quickly with a glass dipped in sugar.

## ALMOND BUTTER COOKIES

1 cup butter or margarine, softened
½ cup sugar
1 cup finely chopped unblanched almonds
2 teaspoons almond extract or vanilla
2 cups all-purpose flour*

Heat oven to 350°. Cream butter and sugar. Stir in almonds and extract. Blend in flour; work with hands until dough is smooth. Shape dough by scant teaspoonfuls into small balls. Place on ungreased baking sheet; flatten slightly. Bake 9 to 10 minutes or until light brown.

*About 6 dozen cookies.*

*°Do not use self-rising flour in this recipe.*

# Have a Roman Holiday

*Some of the nicest parties are family affairs, celebrating nothing in particular. Why not treat your clan to a gala little dinner, à la sunny Italy? Set the table with such trattoria touches as a centerpiece of red and green peppers, candles in jugs or bottles, breadsticks tucked in a mug tied with ribbons of Italian colors. Then serve a Mediterranean menu of Veal Parmesan, Italian beans and a semitropical fruit salad. Light the candles—you're dining out at a favorite restaurant!*

---

*Veal Parmesan*
*Buttered Spaghetti*
*Italian Green Beans*
*Orange-Onion Salad*
*Breadsticks*
*Chocolate Confetti Balls*
*Milk      Coffee*

---

## TIMETABLE

**45 minutes before:**
Prepare and brown veal; cover and simmer

**30 minutes before:**
Make salad; refrigerate

**15 minutes before:**
Cook spaghetti
Set table
Crush wafers for chocolate balls

**10 minutes before:**
Cook green beans
Heat tomato sauce

**Just before serving:**
Drain and butter spaghetti

**Serve main course.**

**Prepare dessert; serve.**

## VEAL PARMESAN

4 veal cutlets (about 4 ounces each)
   or 1-pound veal round steak,
   ½ inch thick
½ cup dry bread crumbs
¼ cup grated Parmesan cheese
½ teaspoon salt
⅛ teaspoon pepper
⅛ teaspoon paprika
1 egg
⅓ cup salad oil
3 tablespoons water
1 can (8 ounces) tomato sauce
½ teaspoon oregano, if desired

If using veal round steak, cut into 4 servings. Pound veal until ¼ inch thick. Stir together bread crumbs, cheese, salt, pepper and paprika. Beat egg slightly. Dip meat into egg, then into crumb mixture, coating both sides.

Heat oil in skillet. Brown meat on both sides, about 6 minutes. Reduce heat. Add water; cover and simmer about 30 minutes or until meat is tender. (If necessary, add small amount of water.) Remove meat from skillet; keep warm. Pour tomato sauce into skillet. Stir in oregano; heat to boiling and pour over spaghetti and meat.

*4 servings.*

## BUTTERED SPAGHETTI

Cook 1 package (6 or 7 ounces) spaghetti as directed. Drain; toss with 3 tablespoons butter or margarine.

*4 servings.*

## ITALIAN GREEN BEANS

Cook 2 packages (9 ounces each) frozen Italian green beans as directed. Stir in 1 tablespoon butter or margarine.

*4 generous servings.*

## ORANGE-ONION SALAD

**2 large oranges**
**1 medium Bermuda onion**
  **Lettuce**
  **Pimiento strips**
  **Favorite fruit salad dressing or**
  **Lemon-Honey Dressing (below)**

Pare oranges; cut crosswise into slices. Peel onion and cut crosswise into thin slices. On 4 lettuce-lined plates, alternate slices of orange and onion. Top each serving with pimiento strips. Serve with fruit salad dressing.

*4 servings.*

### LEMON-HONEY DRESSING

**⅓ cup frozen lemonade or limeade**
  **concentrate (thawed)**
**⅓ cup honey**
**⅓ cup salad oil**
**1 teaspoon celery seed**

Stir together all ingredients.

*1 cup.*

## CHOCOLATE CONFETTI BALLS

**8 cinnamon graham wafers, crushed**
  **(about ½ cup crumbs)**
**1 tablespoon confetti decorators' candies**
**1 pint chocolate ice cream**

Mix crumbs and candies. Scoop ice cream into 4 balls. Roll each in crumb mixture; place in serving dish. Serve immediately or freeze until serving time.

*4 servings.*

**Note:** If cinnamon graham wafers are not available, substitute ½ cup graham cracker crumbs and mix in ¼ teaspoon cinnamon and ½ teaspoon sugar.

### VARIATION
■ *Confetti Snowballs:* Omit wafers and candies. Roll ice-cream balls in tinted coconut. (To tint coconut, place 1 cup flaked coconut and 1 teaspoon red or green sugar in plastic bag or jar. Close tightly and shake until coconut is uniformly colored.)

## APPLEMINT PARFAITS

*Substitute this ice-cream dessert for the Chocolate Confetti Balls if you wish.*

Tint 1 cup applesauce with few drops red or green food color; stir in ½ teaspoon peppermint extract. Alternate layers of vanilla ice cream and applesauce in parfait glasses.

### VARIATIONS
Substitute one of the following for the applesauce and vanilla ice cream:

■ Scoops of lime or orange sherbet alternated with vanilla ice cream
■ Scoops of strawberry ice cream alternated with chocolate and pistachio ice cream

# Hamburger with a Royal Touch

*There are so many ways of serving hamburger you may never get around to all of them. But here's one you won't want to miss. Just 45 minutes from start to finish, this combination of hamburger, noodles Romanoff and mushroom soup has a gourmet flavor that suggests hours in the making. Couple it with vinegary tomatoes and buttered broccoli; then earn special kudos by the simple expedient of warming slices of rye bread before serving. The crowning touch: warm upside-down cake.*

---

*Hamburger Romanoff*
*Buttered Broccoli Spears*
*Tomatoes Vinaigrette*
*Warm Dark Rye Bread*
*Apricot Upside-down Cake*
*Milk      Coffee*

---

## TIMETABLE

**45 minutes before:**
   Heat oven to 350°
   Bake cake

**35 minutes before:**
   Prepare Tomatoes Vinaigrette; refrigerate
   Cook noodles
   Brown meat
   Set table

**15 minutes before:**
   Combine ingredients for Hamburger
      Romanoff; heat to boiling and simmer
   Cook broccoli
   Wrap dark rye bread slices in aluminum
      foil and heat

**5 minutes before:**
   Arrange tomatoes on salad plates

**Serve dinner.**

## HAMBURGER ROMANOFF

1 **pound ground beef**
1 **package (5.5 ounces) noodles
   Romanoff**
1 **can (10½ ounces) condensed cream of
   mushroom soup**
1 **tablespoon instant minced onion**
2 **tablespoons chopped pimiento**

Cook and stir ground beef until brown. Drain off fat. Prepare noodles Romanoff as directed on package except—increase milk to 1 cup. Stir in meat, soup, onion and pimiento. Heat to boiling. Reduce heat; simmer uncovered 10 minutes.

*4 servings.*

**Note:** For 6 servings, use 1½ pounds ground beef, 1 package (8.5 ounces) noodles Romanoff, 1½ cups milk, 2 tablespoons instant minced onion and 3 tablespoons chopped pimiento.

Pineapple Upside-down Cake

## BUTTERED BROCCOLI SPEARS

Cook 2 packages (10 ounces each) frozen broccoli spears as directed. Stir in 1 tablespoon butter or margarine.

*4 generous servings.*

## TOMATOES VINAIGRETTE

Slice 2 or 3 large tomatoes. Place slices in square pan, 9x9x2 inches. Pour ½ cup bottled oil-and-vinegar salad dressing over tomatoes and sprinkle with instant minced onion and parsley flakes. Cover; refrigerate. At serving time, divide slices among 4 lettuce cups and top each with dressing. If desired, sprinkle with oregano leaves.

*4 servings.*

## APRICOT UPSIDE-DOWN CAKE

¼ cup butter or margarine
½ cup brown sugar (packed)
1 can (1 pound 1 ounce) apricot halves, drained
  Maraschino cherries
  Pecan halves
1 package (18.5 ounces) yellow cake mix

Heat oven to 350°. Melt butter over low heat in round layer pan, 9x1½ inches. Sprinkle sugar evenly over butter. Arrange apricot halves, cherries and pecans over sugar mixture.

Prepare cake mix as directed on package. Pour half the batter (about 2½ cups) evenly over fruit in pan. Bake 35 to 45 minutes or until wooden pick inserted in center comes out clean. Invert at once onto serving plate. Leave pan over cake a few minutes. Serve warm and, if desired, with whipped cream.

*9 wedges.*

**Note:** Bake remaining batter in greased and floured 8- or 9-inch round layer pan as directed on package. Use as desired or freeze.

### VARIATIONS

■ *Peach Upside-down Cake:* Substitute 1 can (1 pound 4 ounces) sliced peaches, drained, for the apricot halves.
■ *Pineapple Upside-down Cake:* Substitute 1 can (8½ ounces) pineapple slices, drained, 1 can (13½ ounces) crushed pineapple, drained, or 1 can (13½ ounces) pineapple tidbits, drained, for the apricot halves.

## Timesaver

*Bake 1 package (21.5 ounces) pineapple upside-down cake mix as directed.*

# The Second Time Around

*If leftovers get a chilly reception at your house, don't despair. Here's a way of using up the last of the roast that makes it taste deliciously different from the first go-around. "Stuffing" is layered over slices of pork, moistened with soup and then baked until croutons are brown and hot but celery remains crisp. Want a gelatin salad that sets in 20 minutes? Try our trick of stirring frozen relish into hot gelatin.*

---

*Pork 'n Stuffing Bake*
*Lima Beans and Carrots*
*Cranberry-Orange Salad*
*Warm Fudge Nut Squares*
*Milk      Coffee*

---

### TIMETABLE

**Ahead of time:**
Cut up pork roast

**45 minutes before:**
Heat oven to 350°
Prepare Pork 'n Stuffing Bake

**30 minutes before:**
Place main dish in oven
Make salad; chill
Bake nut squares

**15 minutes before:**
Cook lima beans
Set table

**5 minutes before:**
Add carrots and basil to lima beans; continue cooking
Place salad on lettuce

**Serve main course.**

**Remove nut squares from oven; cut and serve.**

## PORK 'N STUFFING BAKE

3 cups cut-up cooked pork roast
3½ cups herb-seasoned croutons
½ cup diced celery
½ cup chopped onion or
2 tablespoons instant chopped onion
⅓ cup butter or margarine, melted
½ cup water
1 can (10½ ounces) condensed cream of chicken soup
¼ cup water

Heat oven to 350°. Place meat in ungreased square pan, 9x9x2 inches, or 2-quart casserole. For stuffing, combine croutons, celery and onion in bowl. Add butter and ½ cup water; toss until croutons are moistened. Reserve about 1½ cups stuffing; spread remainder over meat. Blend soup and ¼ cup water; pour over stuffing. Top with reserved stuffing. Bake uncovered 30 minutes or until heated through.

*4 to 6 servings.*

### VARIATION
■ *Turkey or Chicken 'n Stuffing Bake:* Substitute 3 cups cut-up cooked turkey or chicken for the pork.

86

## LIMA BEANS AND CARROTS

1 can (1 pound) sliced carrots
1 package (10 ounces) frozen lima beans
⅛ teaspoon basil leaves
2 tablespoons butter or margarine

Drain carrots, reserving liquid. Cook lima beans as directed on package except—substitute ½ cup reserved carrot liquid for the salted water; 5 minutes before end of cooking time, add carrots and basil. Continue cooking until lima beans are tender and carrots are heated through. Stir in butter.

*4 to 6 servings.*

## CRANBERRY-ORANGE SALAD

¾ cup boiling water
1 package (3 ounces) lemon-flavored gelatin
1 package (10 ounces) frozen cranberry-orange relish
Lettuce

Pour boiling water over gelatin in loaf pan, 9x5x3 inches, stirring until gelatin is dissolved. Add frozen cranberry relish to gelatin. Mash and stir relish with fork until thawed. Chill about 20 minutes or until set. Cut into slices and serve on lettuce.

*4 to 6 servings.*

## Timesaver

*The use of still-frozen cranberry-orange relish makes this salad very quick to set. Remember this trick whenever you want a gelatin salad in a hurry. (Maybe you can adapt this method to your own favorite molded salad.)*

## WARM FUDGE NUT SQUARES

1 package (18.5 ounces) devils food cake mix
1 cup chopped nuts
1 package (6 ounces) semisweet chocolate pieces (1 cup)

Heat oven to 350°. Prepare cake mix as directed on package except—pour batter into greased and floured jelly roll pan, 15½x10½x1 inch. Sprinkle nuts and chocolate pieces over batter; bake 25 to 30 minutes. Cool slightly. Cut four to six 3-inch squares. Serve warm (with ice cream or frozen whipped topping if desired). Cut remaining cake into bars and freeze for future use.

## WARM GINGER NUT SQUARES

*To vary the menu, substitute this recipe for the Fudge Nut Squares.*

1 package (14.5 ounces) gingerbread mix
1 cup applesauce
½ cup raisins
½ cup finely chopped nuts

Heat oven to 350°. Grease and flour square pan, 9x9x2 inches. Prepare gingerbread mix as directed on package except—decrease water to ¼ cup and add applesauce. Stir in raisins and nuts. Spread in pan. Bake 35 to 40 minutes. Cut into squares and serve warm.

# Freezer-to-Oven Meal

*This is the kind of freezer-to-oven meal every woman welcomes. Nothing needs to be thawed and everything bakes at the same temperature. The tart shells, if not made ahead of time, go into the oven with the fish, then are removed to cool while the fish continues to bake. Ten minutes before serving time, slip the bread into the oven and arrange the tomato slices on the fish. When it's time for dessert, simply spoon pudding into the tart shells and serve.*

---

*Baked Fish with Mushroom Sauce*
*Hot Cabbage Slaw*
*Parmesan French Bread*
*Lemon Tarts*
*Milk     Coffee*

---

## TIMETABLE

**Ahead of time:**
  Make tart squares and freeze
**45 minutes before:**
  Chill pudding
  Heat oven to 475°
  Prepare fish and frozen tart squares for
    baking
**35 minutes before:**
  Bake fish
  Bake tart squares
  Set table
  Prepare and wrap bread for heating
**20 minutes before:**
  Prepare Hot Cabbage Slaw
  Slice tomatoes
**10 minutes before:**
  Place tomato slices on fish
  Heat bread
**Serve main course.**
**Fill tart shells; serve.**

## BAKED FISH WITH MUSHROOM SAUCE

  2 packages (1 pound each) frozen ocean
    white fish fillets (sole, cod, halibut or
    haddock)
  ½ teaspoon thyme, if desired
  1 can (10½ ounces) condensed cream
    of mushroom soup
  2 small tomatoes
  1 to 2 tablespoons soft butter or
    margarine
    Parsley flakes or dill weed

Heat oven to 475°. Place frozen fish fillets in ungreased baking pan, 13x9x2 inches. Stir thyme into mushroom soup; spread over fish. Bake uncovered 30 minutes. Slice tomatoes; cut each slice in half and place on fish. Brush butter over tomatoes; sprinkle with parsley. Bake uncovered 5 minutes longer or until fish flakes easily with fork.

*6 servings.*

## HOT CABBAGE SLAW

**4 cups coarsely shredded green cabbage**
**1 can (1 pound) cut green beans, drained**
**¼ cup sugar**
**1 tablespoon instant minced onion**
**1 teaspoon salt**
**½ cup vinegar**

Combine all ingredients in 2-quart saucepan. Heat to boiling. Reduce heat; simmer uncovered, tossing occasionally, until cabbage is crisp-tender, about 5 minutes.

*6 servings.*

## PARMESAN FRENCH BREAD

**½ loaf (1 pound) French bread**
**Soft butter or margarine**
**Grated Parmesan cheese**

Heat oven to 475°. Cut bread into six to eight 1-inch slices. Butter slices; sprinkle with cheese. Reassemble ½ loaf; wrap in aluminum foil. Heat in oven 10 minutes.

*6 servings.*

## LEMON TARTS

**1 package (11 ounces) pie crust mix**
**1 can (18 ounces) lemon pudding, chilled**
**Frozen whipped topping**
**6 maraschino cherries**

Prepare pastry for one-crust pie as directed on pie crust mix package except—roll pastry into rectangle, about 11x8 inches. Cut into six 3½-inch squares. Prick each square thoroughly. Stack squares with 4-inch squares of aluminum foil between. Wrap stack in foil; freeze.

To bake: Heat oven to 475°. Invert 6 custard cups on baking sheet. Remove pastry squares from foil; place each frozen square on an inverted custard cup or on alternating muffin cups of 12-cup muffin pan. (Pastry shapes itself around cup during baking.) Bake 8 to 10 minutes. Cool. Remove from cups.

Fill each tart shell with about ⅓ cup lemon pudding; garnish with frozen whipped topping and maraschino cherry.

*6 servings.*

Place frozen pastry on alternating muffin cups.

As it bakes, pastry shapes itself to form tart shell.

# Oriental Express

*A special occasion calls for a special dish—but it needn't mean spending all day in the kitchen. This epicurean main dish, a medley of the tastes and textures of chicken, fruit and vegetables, plus its exotic accompaniments, is ready to serve in just 45 minutes.*

---

*Sweet-sour Chicken*
*Fluffy Rice*
*Chinese Pea Pods*
*Sesame Butter Sticks*
*Melon Balls and Lemon Sherbet*
*Milk     Tea*

---

### TIMETABLE

**Ahead of time:**
   Cut up chicken
**45 minutes before:**
   Thaw melon balls as directed on
      package
   Heat oven to 450°
   Bake Sesame Butter Sticks
**30 minutes before:**
   Drain carrots and pineapple (reserve
      syrup)
   Cut green pepper into squares
   Prepare cut-up chicken and brown
   Set table
**15 minutes before:**
   Finish making main dish
   Cook 1 package (7 ounces) frozen
      Chinese pea pods as directed
**Serve dinner.**

## SWEET-SOUR CHICKEN

   1 egg
2½ cups cut-up cooked chicken
      (about ½-inch pieces)
   ¼ cup cornstarch
   2 tablespoons shortening
   1 can (13½ ounces) pineapple chunks,
      drained (reserve syrup)
   ½ cup vinegar
   ½ cup sugar
   1 medium green pepper, cut into
      1-inch squares
      Instant rice
   ¼ cup water
   2 tablespoons cornstarch
   1 teaspoon soy sauce
   1 can (1 pound) small carrots, drained

Beat egg in medium bowl. Add chicken and toss until coated. Sprinkle with ¼ cup cornstarch; toss until all pieces are coated.

Melt shortening in large skillet. Add chicken; cook until brown. Remove from skillet.

Add enough water to reserved syrup to make 1 cup. Stir liquid, vinegar and sugar into skillet. Heat to boiling, stirring constantly. Stir in green pepper; heat to boiling. Reduce heat; cover and simmer 2 minutes. Cook rice as directed on package for 4 servings.

Blend water and 2 tablespoons cornstarch. Stir into mixture in skillet. Cook, stirring constantly, until mixture thickens and boils. Boil and stir 1 minute. Stir in pineapple, soy sauce, carrots and chicken; heat. Serve over rice.

*4 servings.*

Coat chicken first with egg, then with cornstarch.     Cook chicken pieces in skillet until golden brown.

For a mold as pictured, press 6 cups hot cooked rice into ungreased 1-quart mold; immediately unmold.

Melon Boats with Sherbet

## SESAME BUTTER STICKS

Heat oven to 450°. Melt ⅓ cup butter or margarine in baking pan, 13x9x2 inches, in oven. Mix Biscuit dough as directed on package of buttermilk baking mix; roll dough into rectangle, 10x6 inches. Cut in half lengthwise. Cut each half into 12 strips, each about ¾ inch wide. Dip sticks in melted butter to coat all sides; arrange in single layer in pan. Sprinkle 1 tablespoon sesame seed over sticks. Bake 12 to 15 minutes. Serve hot.

*24 sticks.*

## MELON BALLS AND LEMON SHERBET

**1 pint lemon sherbet**
**1 package (12 ounces) frozen melon balls, thawed and drained**

In each of 4 dessert dishes, place a scoop of sherbet. Spoon melon balls over sherbet.

*4 servings.*

### VARIATIONS

■ *Melon Boats with Sherbet:* Arrange wedges of chilled honeydew or cantaloupe on dessert plates. Top each with a scoop of sherbet.

■ *Pineapple Tidbits with Sherbet:* Omit lemon sherbet and melon balls; divide 1 can (13½ ounces) pineapple tidbits among 4 dessert dishes. Top each with a scoop of lime sherbet.

# A Feast to Grow Slim On

*If someone in the family is a weight-watcher, help the cause along with attractive, appetizing meals that are low in calories. This menu, which totals an unbelievable 371, is guaranteed to satisfy the hungriest dieter. At the same time, it's easily adapted for the non-dieters. For example, the chicken breasts are skinned before cooking to remove most of the fat. Asparagus is zipped up with lemon juice. Diet bread and skim milk cut calories still further, as does the berry dessert with its frozen whipped topping. For non-dieters, don't skin the chicken, add butter to the asparagus, serve whole milk, rolls and whipped cream.*

---

*Golden Baked Chicken*
*Lemon Asparagus*
*Lettuce and Tomato Salad*
*Diet Bread or Crispy Crackers*
*Berry Cloud Dessert*
*Skim Milk     Coffee*

---

## TIMETABLE

**45 minutes before:**
   Heat oven to 425°
   Prepare chicken

**40 minutes before:**
   Put chicken in oven
   Set table

**20 minutes before:**
   Prepare and begin cooking asparagus
   Make salad
   Hull and slice strawberries

**Serve main course.**

**Prepare dessert; serve.**

## GOLDEN BAKED CHICKEN

 2 chicken breasts (about ½ pound each), split
 4 teaspoons soft butter or margarine
 1 to 2 tablespoons instant minced onion
 ½ teaspoon garlic salt
 ¼ teaspoon paprika
 2 tablespoons snipped parsley, if desired

Heat oven to 425°. Remove skin from chicken; place in ungreased baking pan, 8x8x2 or 9x9x2 inches, or 9-inch round baking dish.

Spread 1 teaspoon butter on each piece; sprinkle with onion, garlic salt and paprika. Bake uncovered 35 to 40 minutes. Sprinkle with parsley.

*4 servings.*

## CALORIE CHART

| Food | Amount | Calories (approx.) |
|---|---|---|
| Chicken Breast (no skin) | 3 ounces | 90 |
| Butter | 1 teaspoon | 33 |
| Onion (instant) | 1 teaspoon | 2 (about) |
| Asparagus (fresh) | ½ cup | 20 |
| Lettuce and Tomato Salad | 1 serving | 30 (about) |
| Rye Cracker | 1 | 21 |
| Angel Food Cake (unfrosted) | 1-inch slice | 55 |
| Strawberries (fresh) | ¼ cup | 15 |
| Frozen Whipped Topping | 1 tablespoon | 15 |
| Milk (skim) | 1 cup | 90 |
| | | 371 calories per serving |

## LEMON ASPARAGUS

Break off tough ends from 1 pound fresh asparagus (break off as far down as stalks snap easily). Wash asparagus thoroughly. Remove scales if sandy or tough. (If necessary, remove sand particles with a vegetable brush.)

Fill 10-inch skillet half full of water; add 1 teaspoon salt. Heat water to boiling; add asparagus. Heat to boiling. Cover; cook 8 to 12 minutes or until stalk ends are crisp-tender. Drain; sprinkle with 1 tablespoon lemon juice.

*4 servings.*

**Note:** 1 or 2 packages (10 ounces each) frozen asparagus cuts or spears, cooked as directed on package, or 1 can (15 ounces) asparagus cuts, heated, can be substituted for fresh asparagus.

## LETTUCE AND TOMATO SALAD

**4 lettuce slices, each 1 inch thick**
**1 tomato, cut into 8 wedges, or 8 cherry tomatoes**
**½ cup plain yogurt**
**½ cup chopped pared cucumber**
**½ teaspoon salt**

On each lettuce slice, place 2 tomato wedges. In small bowl, mix remaining ingredients; spoon over lettuce and tomatoes.

*4 servings.*

## BERRY CLOUD DESSERT

For each serving, top a slice of angel food cake with frozen whipped topping and sliced fresh strawberries.

# Please-a-Teen Pizzaburger

*Celebrate a teen-ager's triumph (a berth on the team, a leading role in the play, or a physics exam passed with flying colors) with a dinner that stars Pizzaburger Pie. With a choice of favorite toppings it looks and tastes like pizza, though the "crust" is actually ground beef. Use up leftover frankfurter buns as buttered bun sticks and make the gelatin dessert using our speed-up suggestion. What more could a teen-ager ask?*

*Pizzaburger Pie*
*Endive-Lettuce Salad*
*Buttered Bun Sticks*
*Strawberry Delight*
*Milk      Coffee*

---

### TIMETABLE

**35 minutes before:**
Heat oven to 425°
Prepare Pizzaburger Pie
Heat water for gelatin

**25 minutes before:**
Place Pizzaburger Pie in oven
Make Strawberry Delight; refrigerate

**15 minutes before:**
Make salad
Bake bun sticks
Set table

**Serve dinner.**

## PIZZABURGER PIE

1 **pound ground beef**
½ **cup dry bread crumbs**
½ **teaspoon oregano**
1 **teaspoon salt**
1 **can (8 ounces) tomato sauce**
1 **can (8 ounces) kidney beans, drained**
3 **ounces Cheddar or mozzarella cheese, cut into strips**

Heat oven to 425°. Mix ground beef, bread crumbs, oregano, salt and ½ cup of the tomato sauce. Spread in ungreased 10-inch pizza pan or on bottom and side of 10-inch pie pan. Top with remaining sauce; spread kidney beans over top. Arrange cheese strips in criss-cross design on beans. Bake 20 to 25 minutes.

*4 servings.*

### VARIATIONS
Omit kidney beans and add one of the following:
■ 1 can (2 ounces) mushroom stems and pieces, drained
■ 1 can (7 ounces) vacuum-pack whole kernel corn, drained
■ 1 can (8 ounces) cut green beans, drained
■ ½ medium onion, sliced
■ 1 package (9 ounces) frozen French fried onion rings (2 cups)

Pizzaburger Pie and variations

Stir frozen strawberries into hot gelatin mixture.

Serve Strawberry Delight with whipped topping.

## ENDIVE-LETTUCE SALAD

1 small bunch curly endive,
    washed and chilled
½ small head lettuce, washed and
    chilled
⅓ cup bottled Italian salad dressing
1 small green pepper, cut into rings

Into bowl, tear greens into bite-size pieces (about 5 cups). Add dressing and toss until greens are coated. Garnish with pepper rings.

*4 servings.*

## BUTTERED BUN STICKS

Heat oven to 425°. Cut 3 or 4 split frankfurter buns lengthwise in half. Brush each piece with soft butter or margarine; sprinkle with garlic salt. Place buttered side up on ungreased baking sheet. Bake 5 to 8 minutes or until light brown.

*12 to 16 sticks.*

## STRAWBERRY DELIGHT

1 cup boiling water
1 package (3 ounces) strawberry-flavored
    gelatin
1 package (10 or 16 ounces) frozen
    sliced strawberries
1 large banana
    Vanilla or strawberry yogurt or frozen
    whipped topping

Pour boiling water over gelatin in bowl; stir until gelatin is dissolved. Add frozen strawberries; stir with fork to break berries apart. Slice banana into gelatin and gently stir in. Divide among 4 dessert dishes; chill until serving time. Serve each topped with spoonful of yogurt.

*4 servings.*

### VARIATION

■ *Raspberry Delight:* Substitute 1 package (3 ounces) raspberry-flavored gelatin and 1 package (10 ounces) frozen raspberries for the strawberry-flavored gelatin and frozen strawberries. Top each serving with vanilla or raspberry yogurt.

# Show Off Your New Skillet

*If you're the proud possessor of a new electric skillet, we suggest you christen it suitably with this Pork Chop Dinner-in-a-Dish, then bring it to the table for serving. Chops (extra-thin for quick cooking), canned potatoes and frozen peas cook in the same creamy mushroom sauce, while foil-wrapped rolls warm on top of the range. Here, tangy cider ice serves as dessert but another time you might try it as an unusual meat accompaniment.*

*Pork Chop Dinner-in-a-Dish
Lettuce Tomato Towers
Cloverleaf Rolls
Cider Ice
Marshmallow Bars
Milk     Coffee*

## TIMETABLE

**Ahead of time:**
  Make Cider Ice

**35 minutes before:**
  Brown chops
  While chops are browning, stir together
    soup, mushrooms and seasonings
  Set table

**25 minutes before:**
  Add soup mixture to chops; continue
    cooking
  Make Marshmallow Bars

**10 minutes before:**
  Add pimiento, potatoes and peas to
    skillet and simmer
  Heat rolls
  Make salad

**Serve dinner.**

## PORK CHOP DINNER-IN-A-DISH

2 tablespoons salad oil
8 pork chops, ¼ inch thick
1 can (10½ ounces) condensed cream
  of mushroom soup
1 can (4 ounces) mushroom stems and
  pieces
¼ cup water
½ teaspoon garlic salt
¼ teaspoon thyme
2 tablespoons cooking sherry, if desired
½ teaspoon Worcestershire sauce
1 tablespoon chopped pimiento
1 can (10 ounces) whole potatoes,
  drained
1 package (10 ounces) frozen green
  peas, broken apart

Heat oil in large skillet; cook chops over medium-high heat until brown on both sides. Stir together soup, mushrooms (with liquid), water, garlic salt, thyme, sherry and Worcestershire sauce; pour over meat. Heat to boiling, stirring occasionally. Reduce heat; cover and simmer 10 minutes. Add pimiento, potatoes and peas. Cover; simmer 10 minutes or until potatoes are heated through and peas are tender, stirring occasionally.

*4 servings.*

**Note:** Pork steaks can be substituted for the pork chops. If steaks are ½ inch thick, increase first simmering time to 20 minutes.

99

## LETTUCE TOMATO TOWERS

½ medium head lettuce, washed and
   chilled
2 medium tomatoes
   Favorite oil-and-vinegar salad dressing

Cut lettuce into four ½-inch slices. Cut a thin slice from top and bottom of each tomato, then cut each tomato in half. Place tomato half on each lettuce slice. Serve with salad dressing.

*4 servings.*

## CLOVERLEAF ROLLS

Heat cloverleaf rolls in bun warmer or wrap in aluminum foil and place in saucepan. Cover; place over low heat 10 to 15 minutes or until rolls are hot.

## CIDER ICE

Stir together 2 cups apple cider and ½ cup light corn syrup. Pour into refrigerator tray; freeze until firm around edges and center is mushy, about 2 hours. Remove from freezer; place in chilled small mixer bowl and beat at low speed until mushy. Beat high speed until white and foamy (do not overbeat). Pour into refrigerator tray; freeze until firm.

*4 servings.*

**VARIATION**

■ *Triple Fruit Ice:* Stir ½ cup orange juice and ¼ cup lemon juice into apple cider.

**Note:** Cider Ice and Triple Fruit Ice are delicious as meat accompaniments.

## MARSHMALLOW BARS

⅓ cup butter
32 large marshmallows or 3 cups
   miniature marshmallows
½ teaspoon vanilla
5 cups corn puffs cereal

Butter square pan, 9x9x2 inches. In large saucepan, heat butter and marshmallows over medium-high heat until bubbly. Immediately lower heat and stir constantly until marshmallows are melted. Remove from heat; stir in vanilla. Fold in cereal until evenly coated. Turn into prepared pan. With buttered hands, pat evenly in pan. Cool. Cut into bars, 3x1½ inches.

*18 bars.*

## PEANUT BUTTER CHOCOLATE CHIP BARS

*You can substitute these bars for Marshmallow Bars. Bake them ahead of time or while you are preparing the meal and serve them warm.*

1 package (18.5 ounces) yellow cake mix
⅓ cup water
¼ cup butter or margarine, softened
2 eggs
1 cup crunchy peanut butter
1 package (12 ounces) semisweet
   chocolate pieces

Heat oven to 375°. Grease and flour jelly roll pan, 15½x10½x1 inch. Blend half the cake mix (dry mix), the water, butter, eggs and peanut butter. Mix in remaining cake mix (batter will be stiff). Stir in chocolate pieces. Spread in prepared pan. Bake 20 to 25 minutes. Cut into bars, 3x1½ inches.

*About 30 bars.*

# 50- to 60-Minute Dinners

*Dinner's at 6? Start any one of these delicious meals at 5. While it's cooking, you can take time to relax, give an assist with somebody's homework, sew a button on Junior's jacket or make a quick phone call. Your kitchen timer is a big asset here—it keeps everything under control.*

# Shortcut with a Blender

*A delicious and unusual medley of pork chops, onions and sweet potatoes simmers in orange juice in a skillet while dessert bakes in the oven. Meanwhile, you can prepare cabbage for coleslaw, almost instantly, in a blender. Don't overblend—three or four seconds does it.*

---

*Orange Pork Chop Skillet*
*Buttered Green Peas and Mushrooms*
*Creamy Coleslaw*
*Spice Velvet Crumb Cake*
*with Broiled Topping*
*Milk      Coffee*

---

## TIMETABLE

**One hour before:**
 Heat oven to 350°
 Brown pork chops
 Make orange sauce; pour over chops
  and continue cooking

**45 minutes before:**
 Bake cake
 Prepare ingredients for coleslaw;
  refrigerate

**20 minutes before:**
 Arrange potatoes and orange slices
  on chops
 Set table

**15 minutes before:**
 Cook peas
 Mix Broiled Topping

**5 minutes before:**
 Stir mushrooms and butter into peas;
  heat through
 Mix coleslaw

**Serve main course.**

**Spread Broiled Topping on warm cake;**
 broil and serve.

## ORANGE PORK CHOP SKILLET

*Pictured on preceding page.*

**6 pork chops, ½ inch thick**
**1 teaspoon salt**
**1 medium onion, cut into 6 slices**
**1 can (6 ounces) frozen orange juice**
 **concentrate, partially thawed**
**¼ cup brown sugar (packed)**
**½ teaspoon allspice**
**3 tablespoons lemon juice**
**¾ cup water**
**1 can (1 pound 7 ounces) vacuum-pack**
 **sweet potatoes, drained**
**6 thin orange slices**

Trim excess fat from chops; grease, 12-inch skillet with fat. Brown chops on both sides. Season with salt. Drain off fat. Top each chop with an onion slice. Stir together orange juice concentrate, sugar, allspice, lemon juice and water; pour into skillet. Heat to boiling. Reduce heat; cover and simmer 25 minutes. Arrange sweet potatoes and orange slices on chops. Cover; cook 15 minutes longer or until potatoes are heated through.

*4 to 6 servings.*

Coleslaw is ready in seconds when you use a blender.

## CREAMY COLESLAW

1 small green cabbage, cut into 1-inch
  pieces
½ green pepper, cut up
½ cup mayonnaise or salad dressing
¼ cup dairy sour cream
2 teaspoons lemon juice
½ teaspoon salt
¼ teaspoon dry mustard
  Dash pepper

Fill blender container to top-cup marking with vegetables. Add cold water just to cover vegetables. Cover container; follow manufacturer's instructions or run just long enough to chop vegetables, about 3 to 4 seconds. Pour mixture into strainer; drain thoroughly. Repeat with remaining vegetables. Refrigerate.

Mix mayonnaise, sour cream, lemon juice, salt, mustard and pepper. Just before serving, pour over chopped cabbage and green pepper; mix.

*4 to 6 servings.*

**Note:** If you don't have a blender, shred cabbage and chop green pepper. Mix with remaining ingredients.

## BUTTERED GREEN PEAS AND MUSHROOMS

Cook 1 package (10 ounces) frozen green peas as directed. Drain 1 can (4 ounces) mushroom stems and pieces. Stir mushrooms and 1 tablespoon butter or margarine into peas; heat through.

*4 to 6 servings.*

## SPICE VELVET CRUMB CAKE WITH BROILED TOPPING

1½ cups buttermilk baking mix*
½ cup sugar
1 egg
½ cup cold water or milk*
2 tablespoons shortening
1½ teaspoons pumpkin pie spice
1 teaspoon vanilla
  Broiled Topping (below)

Heat oven to 350°. Grease and flour square pan, 8x8x2 inches, or round layer pan, 9x1½ inches. In large mixer bowl, blend all ingredients except Broiled Topping on low speed ½ minute, scraping side and bottom of bowl frequently. Beat 4 minutes medium speed. Pour into prepared pan. Bake 30 to 35 minutes or until wooden pick inserted in center comes out clean. While warm, spread with Broiled Topping.

*°In altitudes over 4,000 feet, add 2 tablespoons flour and increase liquid to ⅔ cup. Bake at 375° 25 to 30 minutes.*

### BROILED TOPPING

Mix 3 tablespoons soft butter or margarine, ⅓ cup brown sugar (packed), 2 tablespoons light cream, ½ cup coconut and ¼ cup chopped nuts. Set oven control at broil and/or 550°. Broil cake about 3 inches from heat about 3 minutes or until golden brown.

**Note:** A 9-inch square pan can be used. Bake cake 25 to 30 minutes.

103

# Have Foil, Will Travel

*Are there new neighbors moving in next door? A nearby friend down with the flu or hobbling on a sprained ankle? Here's your chance to play angel of mercy by arriving on the scene with tasty, hot little dinners, cooked and transported in aluminum foil. The foil will hold the heat while they travel. (The chicken and vegetables in mushroom sauce and the cinnamon candy apples can be made up as far ahead as the night before, sealed in their aluminum "dishes," then refrigerated until you are ready to bake. Then add 10 minutes to the baking time.) Even when there is no emergency, these pot-and-panless dinners are great for the patio or for family dinners on nights when there is a good possibility some member of the family will be arriving home late.*

---

*Little Chicken Dinners in Foil*
*Bread 'n Butter Fingers*
*Relishes*
*Cinnamon Candy Apples*
*Milk     Coffee*

---

### TIMETABLE

**One hour before:**
Heat oven to 450°
Prepare chicken dinners; bake

**50 minutes before:**
Bake Cinnamon Candy Apples

**10 minutes before:**
Arrange ripe olives, sliced pickles and
   cherry tomatoes in serving dish
Make Bread 'n Butter Fingers

**Serve dinner.**

## LITTLE CHICKEN DINNERS IN FOIL

1 package (10 ounces) frozen green peas
4 medium carrots
4 medium potatoes, pared
8 chicken drumsticks or 4 thighs
1 can (10½ ounces) condensed cream
   of mushroom soup
1 envelope (about 1½ ounces) onion
   soup mix

Heat oven to 450°. Place frozen peas in colander or sieve; run cold tap water over peas just until broken apart. Drain.

Tear off 4 pieces heavy-duty aluminum foil, each 18x15 inches. On center of each piece, place 1 carrot, thinly sliced, 1 potato, cut into quarters, and 2 drumsticks. Stir together mushroom soup and onion soup mix; spoon soup mixture over drumsticks and top with peas. Wrap securely in foil; place on ungreased baking sheet. Bake 50 minutes or until chicken is tender.

*4 servings.*

## LITTLE BEEF DINNERS IN FOIL

*If your family likes beef better than chicken, have these instead of the Little Chicken Dinners.*

Follow recipe for Little Chicken Dinners in Foil (page 104) except—omit chicken and substitute 1 to 1½ pounds ½-inch-thick beef round steak cut into 1-inch pieces. Divide meat pieces among the 4 packets. If desired, 2 packages (10 ounces each) frozen peas and carrots can be substituted for the frozen peas and fresh carrots.

## BREAD 'N BUTTER FINGERS

Spread 6 slices bread with soft butter or margarine; put together to make 3 sandwiches. If desired, add a crisp lettuce leaf to each sandwich. Cut sandwiches into thirds.

*9 fingers.*

## CINNAMON CANDY APPLES

Heat oven to 450°. Wash and core 4 baking apples. Place each on a 12-inch square of heavy-duty aluminum foil. Spoon 2 tablespoons red cinnamon candies into each cavity. Wrap apples securely in foil. Place on ungreased baking sheet. Bake 40 minutes or until soft.

*4 servings.*

## BANANA BOATS

*Substitute this dessert occasionally for Cinnamon Candy Apples and adjust Timetable.*

For each serving, cut a V-shape wedge lengthwise in peeled firm banana. Place on 18x6-inch piece of heavy-duty aluminum foil. Fill groove with cut-up or miniature marshmallows or marshmallow crème and chocolate pieces. Wrap securely in foil. Bake in 450° oven 10 minutes.

## BLUSHING PEACH DESSERT

*This dessert can be substituted for Cinnamon Candy Apples; adjust Timetable.*

For each serving, fill cavity of a well-drained canned peach half with 2 teaspoons red cinnamon candies and 1 teaspoon *each* chopped nuts and lemon juice. Place another peach half cut side down on top. Wrap whole peach securely in 8-inch square of heavy-duty aluminum foil. Bake in 450° oven 15 minutes or until heated through.

## HOT 'N SWEET GRAPEFRUIT

*Vary the menu by substituting this dessert for Cinnamon Candy Apples; adjust Timetable.*

For each serving, seed, section and remove center from a grapefruit half. Place on 12-inch square of heavy-duty aluminum foil. Pour 1 teaspoon honey over fruit; sprinkle with ¼ teaspoon nutmeg. Wrap securely in foil. Bake in 450° oven 20 minutes or until heated through.

# Spareribs and Sauerkraut on the Double

*Is yours a family of sauerkraut fans? Then feed them their favorite fare in either of these two quick-cooking ways. If you have a pressure cooker, spareribs, potatoes and vegetable can cook with the kraut in half the usual time. If not, try an alternate version: Kraut and packaged scalloped potatoes simmer gently for flavor blending, are topped with smoky pork sausage links. An additional vegetable adds balance to the meal. Whichever dish you choose, don't forget traditional go-alongs—dark rye bread and a Waldorf salad dessert. Keep the refrigerated cookie dough on hand to slice and bake as needed.*

---

*Sparerib Sauerkraut Dinner
or Sausage Sauerkraut Dinner
Dark Rye Rolls
Cinnamon Cookies
Dessert Waldorf
Milk      Coffee*

---

## TIMETABLE

**Ahead of time:**
  Prepare cookie dough; chill
**One hour before:**
  Prepare Sparerib Sauerkraut Dinner;
    cook as directed
  Heat oven to 400°
**40 minutes before:**
  Bake cookies
  Prepare Dessert Waldorf
**About 12 minutes before:**
  Wrap rolls in aluminum foil and heat
    in oven
  Set table
**Serve dinner.**

106

## SPARERIB SAUERKRAUT DINNER

3½ pounds spareribs, cut up
 1 jar (1 quart) sauerkraut, drained, or
   2 cans (16 ounces each) sauerkraut,
   drained (reserve liquid)
 5 or 6 medium potatoes, pared and
   halved
 5 or 6 carrots, cut into 2-inch pieces
 1 teaspoon salt

In 6-quart pressure cooker, layer spareribs,° sauerkraut, potatoes and carrots. Season with salt. (Cooker should be no more than about ⅔ full.) Measure reserved sauerkraut liquid and add water to measure 1 cup. Pour into cooker. Seal cooker and process as directed by manufacturer.

*4 to 6 servings.*

°*To brown ribs before cooking, melt 2 tablespoons shortening in pressure cooker. Add spareribs and brown on both sides.*

**Note:** For variety, stir ½ teaspoon caraway seed, ¼ cup brown sugar (packed) and ¼ cup chopped onion into sauerkraut.

Add caraway, brown sugar and onion to sauerkraut.

Layer spareribs and vegetables in pressure cooker.

## SAUSAGE SAUERKRAUT DINNER

1 package (5.5 ounces) scalloped potatoes
1 can (1 pound) sauerkraut, drained
   (reserve liquid)
½ teaspoon caraway seed
1 package (12 ounces) fully cooked
   smoked pork sausage links

Empty potato slices and packet of seasoned sauce mix into 10-inch skillet. Add amount of water called for on package. Add enough water to reserved sauerkraut liquid to measure ⅔ cup; stir liquid, sauerkraut and caraway seed into potatoes. Heat to boiling, stirring occasionally. Reduce heat; cover and simmer 30 minutes or until potatoes are tender. Arrange sausages on top. Cover and cook 10 minutes longer or until sausages are heated through.

*4 to 6 servings.*

**Note:** Include another vegetable in the meal if you're making the sausage main dish.

## CINNAMON COOKIES

1 cup butter or margarine, softened
½ cup granulated sugar
½ cup brown sugar (packed)
2 eggs
3 teaspoons cinnamon
3 cups all-purpose flour*
1 teaspoon salt

Mix thoroughly butter, sugars, eggs and cinnamon. Stir in flour and salt. Divide dough into 3 parts; shape each part into roll, 1½ inches in diameter and about 7 inches long. Wrap; chill at least 4 hours.

Heat oven to 400°. Cut rolls into ⅛-inch slices. Place 1 inch apart on ungreased baking sheet. Bake 8 to 10 minutes. Immediately remove from baking sheet.

*7 dozen cookies.*

## DESSERT WALDORF

2 medium apples
2 teaspoons lemon juice
¼ cup chopped pitted dates
1 cup seedless green grapes
1 can (13½ ounces) pineapple chunks,
   drained
1 cup miniature marshmallows
¼ cup chopped nuts
⅓ cup mayonnaise
⅓ cup dairy sour cream

Thinly slice unpared apples into bowl. Sprinkle lemon juice over apples; toss. Add dates, grapes, pineapple, marshmallows and nuts. Stir together mayonnaise and sour cream. Pour over fruits; mix until fruits are coated. Chill.

*4 to 6 servings.*

### VARIATIONS

■ Substitute 1 cup Tokay grapes, halved and seeded, for the green grapes.

■ Substitute 1 can (8 ounces) green grapes for the fresh grapes.

■ Substitute 1 medium banana, sliced, for the green grapes.

■ Substitute 1 can (11 ounces) mandarin orange segments for the pineapple chunks.

*°If using self-rising flour, omit salt.*

# Skillful Skillet

*The versatile electric skillet cooks this main dish of pork chops and scalloped potatoes to a delicious turn, and brings the food to the table piping hot. Spinach takes on a surprise flavor with instant onion or pearl onions, biscuits are crusted with poppy seed, and the dessert, made from apple pie filling, is topped with crisp sweet butter crunch. Noteworthy notion: Why not make a double order of the butter crunch and use another day as a sundae topping? You'll be glad you did the next time you need a dessert in a hurry!*

---

*Pork Chop Scallop*
*Spinach and Onions*
*Vegetable Relishes*
*Poppy Seed Biscuits*
*Apple Crunch*
*Milk     Coffee*

---

## TIMETABLE

**Ahead of time:**
  Make Butter Crunch; cool and refrigerate
**1 hour before:**
  Prepare vegetable relishes; refrigerate
  Brown pork chops; remove from skillet
**45 minutes before:**
  Prepare Pork Chop Scallop; cover and
    simmer
  Set table
**20 minutes before:**
  Heat oven to 450°
  Prepare Apple Crunch
  Bake biscuits
  Cook spinach
**Serve dinner.**

## PORK CHOP SCALLOP

**4 pork chops, ½ inch thick**
  **Salt and pepper**
**1 package (5.5 ounces) scalloped potatoes**
**2 tablespoons chopped pimiento,**
  **if desired**

Trim excess fat from chops; grease 10-inch skillet with fat. Brown chops on both sides. Season with salt and pepper. Remove chops from skillet. Empty potatoes and packet of seasoned sauce mix into skillet. Stir in pimiento and amounts of water and milk called for on package. Heat to boiling, stirring occasionally. Reduce heat; place pork chops on top. Cover; simmer 30 to 35 minutes or until potatoes are tender. If desired, garnish with parsley.

*4 servings.*

**109**

## SPINACH AND ONIONS

Cook 1 or 2 packages (10 ounces) frozen chopped spinach as directed except—add 1 or 2 tablespoons instant chopped onion to spinach before cooking.

**Note:** If desired, substitute pickled pearl onions for the instant chopped onion.

*4 servings.*

## POPPY SEED BISCUITS

Make Drop Biscuits as directed on package of buttermilk baking mix except—before baking, sprinkle tops with poppy seed.

### VARIATIONS

Omit poppy seed and sprinkle tops of biscuits with one of the following:

- Celery seed
- Snipped or freeze-dried chives
- Onion salt or garlic salt
- Sesame seed

- *Cranberry Surprise Biscuits:* Drop dough by 12 tablespoonfuls onto greased baking sheet; omit poppy seed. Press floured thumb into center of each mound of dough. Fill each hole with ½ teaspoon cranberry jelly; drop remaining dough by teaspoonfuls onto jelly.

- *Cheese Purses:* Drop dough by spoonfuls into 12 greased muffin cups; omit poppy seed. Push half-inch cube of sharp cheese into center of each mound of dough. Bake 10 to 15 minutes or until light brown.

## APPLE CRUNCH

   Butter Crunch (below)
 1 can (1 pound 5 ounces) apple pie filling
 1 teaspoon lemon juice
 ½ teaspoon cinnamon
 1 or 2 drops aromatic bitters, if desired

Prepare Butter Crunch. Heat oven to 450°. Combine remaining ingredients; mix thoroughly. Place apple mixture in ungreased 9-inch pie pan or baking dish, 8x8x2 inches. Sprinkle 1 cup of the Butter Crunch evenly over top. Bake 10 minutes or until top is light golden and bubbly. Serve warm (with ice cream, if desired).

*4 servings.*

### BUTTER CRUNCH

 ½ cup butter or margarine, softened
 ¼ cup brown sugar (packed)
 1 cup all-purpose flour
 ½ cup chopped pecans, walnuts or flaked coconut

Heat oven to 400°. Mix all ingredients with hands. Spread in ungreased baking pan, 13x9x2 inches. Bake 15 minutes. Stir baked mixture with spoon. Cool. Store in covered container in refrigerator for future use.

*2 cups.*

# Let's Celebrate!

*Even a great occasion—birthday, promotion or graduation—can be fittingly celebrated without spending the whole day in the kitchen or the whole evening cleaning up. Chicken comes out of the oven as crisp as any panfried poultry, courtesy of its coating; biscuits bake along in the same pan. And, has it ever occurred to you that frozen vegetables such as squash and beans can cook as easily in oven heat as on top of the range? Well, they can. What's more, they go right from oven to table in their baking dishes. If your celebration is a birthday, serve the dessert sundaes with a candle in each.*

---

*Oven-fried Chicken with Biscuits*
*Zesty Squash      Buttered Green Beans*
*Cranberry Sundaes*
*Milk      Coffee*

---

## TIMETABLE

**One hour before:**
  Heat oven to 425°
  Prepare chicken

**50 minutes before:**
  Bake chicken
  Prepare frozen vegetables for baking

**45 minutes before:**
  Put vegetables in oven
  Set table
  Mix biscuits

**15 minutes before:**
  Drop biscuits in pan with chicken
  Stir squash and green beans
  Heat cranberry-orange relish over low
    heat; keep warm

**Serve main course.**

**Make sundaes; serve.**

## OVEN-FRIED CHICKEN WITH BISCUITS

  2½- to 3-pound broiler-fryer chicken,
  cut up
¼ cup shortening
¼ cup butter or margarine
½ cup buttermilk baking mix
1 teaspoon salt
1 teaspoon paprika
¼ teaspoon pepper
  Biscuit dough

Heat oven to 425°. Wash chicken and pat dry. In oven, melt shortening and butter in baking pan, 13x9x2 inches. Mix baking mix, salt, paprika and pepper; coat chicken. Place chicken skin side down in shortening and butter. Bake 35 minutes.

Make Biscuit dough as directed on package of buttermilk baking mix. Turn chicken, pushing pieces to one side of pan. Drop dough by spoonfuls into pan in single layer next to chicken. Bake 15 minutes longer or until biscuits are light brown and chicken is tender.

*4 servings.*

## ZESTY SQUASH

2 packages (10 ounces each) frozen
   cooked squash
2 tablespoons butter or margarine
½ teaspoon salt
2 tablespoons instant minced onion

Heat oven to 425°. Place frozen squash in ungreased 1½-quart casserole. Dot with butter
and sprinkle with salt. Cover; bake 30 minutes. Stir onion into squash. Cover and bake
10 minutes longer or until squash is heated
through.

*4 generous servings.*

## BUTTERED GREEN BEANS

2 packages (10 ounces each) frozen
   cut green beans
1 teaspoon seasoned salt
¼ cup water
2 tablespoons butter or margarine

Heat oven to 425°. Place frozen beans in
ungreased 1½-quart casserole. Sprinkle salt
and water over beans; dot with butter. Cover;
bake 30 minutes. Stir beans with fork to break
apart; cover and bake 15 minutes longer.

*4 generous servings.*

## Timesaver

*Whenever possible, bake vegetables in the
oven with the main dish—then serve them in
the baking casserole. Other frozen vegetables
such as peas and carrots, mixed vegetables,
asparagus or succotash can be heated this way.*

Cranberry Sundae Jubilee

## CRANBERRY SUNDAES

Heat 1 package (10 ounces) frozen cranberry-
orange relish or 1 can (8 ounces) whole cranberry sauce, stirring occasionally. Place scoop
of vanilla ice cream in each of 4 serving
dishes. Spoon hot relish over ice cream.

*4 servings.*

### VARIATION

■ *Cranberry Sundaes Jubilee:* Soak 4 sugar
cubes in orange extract 5 to 10 minutes. Just
before serving, place a cube on top of each
sundae and ignite.

**Note:** For a special occasion, serve in parfait
glasses or other attractive stemmed glassware.

114

# Starring the Barbecue

*A backyard barbecue grill sets the stage. And the whole family pitches in to help with the food while the coals are heating. The flank steak is tenderized with a garlic and oregano marinade, then basted with tomato sauce as it cooks. Rolls and corn share the grill with the meat and frozen waffles for the dessert shortcakes heat over the coals while the steak does a disappearing act at the table.*

---

*Barbecued Steak*
*Corn on the Cob*
*Tossed Pea Salad*
*Grilled Rolls*
*Jiffy Strawberry Shortcakes*
*Milk      Iced Tea*

---

## TIMETABLE

**About 1 hour before:**
Heat grill
Prepare steak; refrigerate
Thaw frozen strawberries
Prepare ingredients for salad; refrigerate
Stir sugar into topping; refrigerate
Wrap corn for grilling
Split rolls and butter

**20 minutes before:**
Start grilling corn
Set up table service

**10 minutes before:**
Start broiling steak

**5 minutes before:**
Turn steak
Heat rolls on grill
Toss salad

**Serve main course.**

**Prepare desserts and serve.**

## BARBECUED STEAK

2 pounds flank steak or round steak, ½ inch thick
1 teaspoon oregano leaves
1½ teaspoons garlic salt
3 tablespoons salad oil
2 tablespoons vinegar or lemon juice
1 can (8 ounces) tomato sauce

Score surface ⅛ inch deep in diamond design. Place steak in shallow pan. Mix oregano leaves, garlic salt and oil; spread on steak. Drizzle vinegar over steak.

If desired, steak can be tenderized with instant meat tenderizer as directed on package. Cover pan with aluminum foil; refrigerate 1 hour or longer.

Open can of tomato sauce and place at edge of grill to warm. Place steak on grill 4 inches from hot coals. Grill about 5 minutes on each side, basting frequently with tomato sauce. To serve, cut steak diagonally across the grain into thin slices.

*5 or 6 servings.*

## CORN ON THE COB

Remove husks and silk from 5 or 6 fresh ears of corn or use frozen ears of corn. Place each ear on piece of heavy-duty aluminum foil; add 1 tablespoon butter and 1 ice cube or 2 tablespoons water. Wrap securely in foil, twisting ends to make handles for turning. Place on grill 4 inches from hot coals. Grill 20 minutes or until done, turning once.

*5 or 6 servings.*

## TOSSED PEA SALAD

1 package (10 ounces) frozen green
  peas
1 small head lettuce, washed and chilled
10 to 12 radishes, sliced
⅓ cup bottled Italian salad dressing

Place frozen peas in colander or sieve; run hot tap water over peas just until broken apart. Drain.

Into bowl, tear lettuce into bite-size pieces (about 6 cups). Add radishes and peas. Pour salad dressing over vegetables; toss.

*5 or 6 servings.*

**Note:** Here's a handy checklist of items to have on hand at the grill:

- Long-handled tongs (one for the coals and one for the food)
- Asbestos mitts or gloves for hot items
- Basting brush
- Heavy-duty aluminum foil
- Paper towels
- Large serving spoons
- Cutting board for carving
- Carving knife and fork
- Salt and pepper

## GRILLED ROLLS

Split 5 or 6 hard dinner rolls horizontally. Spread cut surfaces with soft butter or margarine. Place halves on grill 4 inches from hot coals. Grill 2 to 3 minutes on each side or until golden brown.

*5 or 6 servings.*

## JIFFY STRAWBERRY SHORTCAKES

1 or 2 tablespoons brown sugar
1 cup frozen whipped topping
5 or 6 frozen small waffles
1 package (16 ounces) frozen sliced
  strawberries, thawed, or 1 quart fresh
  strawberries, sliced

Stir together sugar and whipped topping. Place waffles on grill 4 inches from low coals. Grill 3 to 4 minutes on each side or until crisp. Spoon berries over each waffle and top with sugar-topping mixture.

*5 or 6 servings.*

**Note:** Ice cream or dairy sour cream can be substituted for the sugar and frozen whipped topping.

### VARIATIONS

- *Jiffy Shortcakes:* Substitute 1 can (1 pound 5 ounces) blueberry, cherry, peach or pineapple pie filling for the strawberries.

- *Jiffy Peach Shortcakes:* Substitute 1 package (16 ounces) frozen sliced peaches, thawed, or 1 can (1 pound) sliced peaches, drained, for the strawberries.

- *Jiffy Cranberry Shortcakes:* Substitute 1 can (16 ounces) whole cranberry sauce for the strawberries.

116

A small scoop is convenient for pouring batter.

Let inverted puffs cool slightly on wire rack.

Serve Cranberry Puffs warm with Butter Sauce.

# Easy-Does-It Casserole

*A quick-to-make oven meal can really save the day for a busy homemaker, particularly when everything bakes at the same temperature, as does this meal. The main dish is a delicious casserole of ham, au gratin potatoes and chopped broccoli. The vegetable relishes chill in the refrigerator while you make the tender little Cranberry Puffs, pop them into the oven and fix the tomatoes. Ten minutes before serving, slip the tomatoes into the oven, make the dessert sauce and— "Dinner's ready!"*

*Ham and Broccoli au Gratin*
*Baked Tomatoes*
*Crisp Vegetable Relishes*
*Cranberry Puffs*
*Butter Sauce*
*Milk     Coffee*

---

## TIMETABLE

**One hour before:**
Heat oven to 400°
Prepare Ham and Broccoli au Gratin

**50 minutes before:**
Put main dish in oven
Prepare vegetable relishes; place in bowl of ice and water
Bake Cranberry Puffs
Prepare tomatoes
Set table

**10 minutes before:**
Put tomatoes in oven
Make Butter Sauce (keep warm or reheat just before serving)

**Just before serving:**
Arrange vegetable relishes in serving dish

**Serve dinner.**

## HAM AND BROCCOLI AU GRATIN

1 package (5.5 ounces) au gratin potatoes
1 package (10 ounces) frozen chopped broccoli, partially thawed and broken apart
1½ to 2 cups cut-up cooked ham or 1 can (12 ounces) pork luncheon meat, cut up

Heat oven to 400°.

Prepare potatoes as directed on package except—use 2-quart casserole; omit butter; stir in broccoli and ham and bake uncovered 45 to 50 minutes.

*4 or 5 servings.*

### VARIATIONS
Before baking, stir in one of the following:

- 2 tablespoons thinly sliced green onion
- ¼ cup chopped green pepper
- 1 jar (2 ounces) sliced pimiento, drained
- 1 tablespoon prepared mustard
- ¼ cup sliced pitted ripe olives
- ¼ cup sliced pimiento-stuffed olives
- 1 can (3 ounces) sliced mushrooms, drained

119

## BAKED TOMATOES

4 or 5 medium tomatoes
⅛ teaspoon sage
⅛ teaspoon dry mustard
2 teaspoons soft butter or margarine
  Salt and pepper

Heat oven to 400°. Cut a thin slice from stem end of each tomato. Place unpeeled tomatoes cut side up in ungreased baking dish, 8x8x2 or 9x9x2 inches. Stir together sage, mustard and butter. Spread about ½ teaspoon butter mixture over cut side of each tomato. Season with salt and pepper. Bake 10 to 15 minutes.

*4 or 5 servings.*

## CRISP VEGETABLE RELISHES

Prepare your choice of any of the following relishes; place the fresh vegetables in bowl of ice and water until serving time.

■ *Carrot, Cucumber or Zucchini Sticks:* Cut carrot, cucumber or zucchini into short narrow sticks. If desired, place sticks in pitted ripe olives.

■ *Celery Fans:* Cut celery into sticks and make parallel cuts on one end of each stick.

■ *Radish Fans:* Make thin parallel cuts on side of radish to about ¼ inch of other side.

■ *Broccoli Buds or Cauliflowerets:* Break or cut broccoli or cauliflower into bite-size flowerets.

■ *Cucumber Petals:* Run sharp-tined fork down the length of an unpared cucumber. Cut into thin crosswise slices.

■ *Green Onions:* Trim off green tops, leaving about 2 inches. Cut off root ends and remove loose skin.

## CRANBERRY PUFFS

1 cup cranberry-orange relish
1 cup buttermilk baking mix
¼ cup sugar
1 egg
⅓ cup milk
  Butter Sauce (below)

Heat oven to 400°. Generously grease bottoms of 8 or 9 muffin cups. Spoon about 2 tablespoons cranberry-orange relish into each muffin cup. Mix baking mix, sugar, egg and milk; beat vigorously ½ minute. Fill muffin cups ⅔ full. Bake about 15 minutes or until golden brown. Invert puffs onto wire rack. Serve warm with Butter Sauce.

*8 or 9 puffs.*

### BUTTER SAUCE

Heat ½ cup sugar and ¼ cup light cream to boiling, stirring constantly. Remove from heat. With rotary beater, beat in ¼ cup butter or margarine and ½ teaspoon vanilla.

**Note:** Butter Sauce is also good served over any of the following: date or plum puddings; gingerbread; cottage pudding; yellow or spice cake; vanilla ice cream.

### VARIATION

■ *Cranberry Cake:* Spread cranberry-orange relish in greased square pan, 8x8x2 inches; pour batter over relish and bake 20 to 25 minutes. Cut into squares.

*9 squares.*

# When the Pressure's On

*There's nothing like a pressure cooker to speed up the cooking of foods that traditionally simmer for hours. For example, a hearty country-style chicken stew with potatoes, onions and carrots can be done in an hour, including preparation time. Serve it in big bowls with hot buttered French bread for dunking in the delicious broth and a wilted spinach and lettuce salad sprinkled with bacony little bits. Making the dessert turnovers king-size is a timesaver as well as a conversation piece.*

---

*Chicken Provincial*
*Wilted Double Green Salad*
*Hot Buttered French Bread*
*Jumbo Strawberry Turnovers*
*Milk     Coffee*

---

### TIMETABLE

**One hour before:**
  Prepare Chicken Provincial; cook as
    directed
**40 minutes before:**
  Heat oven to 425°
  Bake turnovers
**20 minutes before:**
  Set table
  Slice French bread. Butter; wrap in
    aluminum foil and heat in oven
    about 10 minutes
  Make salad
  Glaze turnovers
**Serve dinner.**

## CHICKEN PROVINCIAL

  2  **broiler-fryer chickens (2½ pounds
     each), cut up**
  1  **tablespoon plus 1 teaspoon
     seasoned salt**
  ½  **teaspoon seasoned pepper**
  ½  **teaspoon paprika**
  6  **carrots, halved**
  6  **small potatoes, pared**
  6  **small onions**
1¼  **cups water**
1½  **teaspoons parsley flakes
     French bread or hard rolls**

Wash chicken; place in 6-quart pressure cooker. Sprinkle with seasoned salt, seasoned pepper and paprika. Place vegetables on chicken; add water. (Cooker should be no more than about ⅔ full.) Seal cooker and process as directed by manufacturer.

Remove cover; skim fat from broth. Divide chicken, vegetables and broth among 6 soup bowls; sprinkle ¼ teaspoon parsley flakes over each serving. Serve with thick slices of French bread.

*6 servings.*

**Note:** To brown chicken before cooking, melt 2 tablespoons shortening in pressure cooker. Add chicken and brown on all sides.

121

## WILTED DOUBLE GREEN SALAD

8 ounces spinach, washed and chilled
Small head Boston lettuce or 1 bunch
leaf lettuce, washed and chilled
2 teaspoons sugar
¼ cup vinegar
2 tablespoons water
1 tablespoon salad oil
1 teaspoon salt
Dash pepper
2 tablespoons bacon-flavored vegetable
protein chips

Just before serving, tear greens into bite-size pieces (about 8 cups) into bowl. In small saucepan, heat sugar, vinegar, water, salad oil, salt and pepper to boiling. Pour over greens and toss. Sprinkle chips over greens.

*6 servings.*

### VARIATIONS

■ Add ⅓ cup chopped green onion

■ Substitute 8 cups shredded leaf lettuce for the greens.

■ Add ½ teaspoon dill weed and ½ teaspoon dry mustard to the sugar-vinegar mixture.

■ Omit water, salad oil and chips. Fry 8 slices bacon, diced, until crisp; pour off all but 2 tablespoons bacon drippings. Add sugar, vinegar, salt and pepper. Remove from heat; add greens and toss until wilted.

## Timesaver

*Substitute ⅓ cup bottled Italian salad dressing for the sugar, vinegar, water, salad oil, salt and pepper.*

## JUMBO STRAWBERRY TURNOVERS

1 package (11 ounces) pie crust mix
1⅓ cups strawberry preserves
Frosty Glaze (below)

Heat oven to 425°. Prepare pastry for Two-crust Pie as directed on package except—roll half of pastry into 10-inch circle; place on ungreased baking sheet. Spread ⅔ cup of the preserves on half of circle to within ½ inch of edge. Fold pastry over; press edges firmly with fork to seal securely. Cut slits in top. Repeat with remaining pastry. Bake 12 to 15 minutes or until golden brown. While warm, frost with Frosty Glaze. Cut each turnover into 3 wedges. Serve warm.

*6 servings.*

### FROSTY GLAZE

Blend ½ cup confectioners' sugar, 1 tablespoon soft butter and 1 tablespoon milk.

## PINEAPPLE-ORANGE CRUNCH

*Substitute this for the Jumbo Strawberry Turnovers if you like and adjust Timetable.*

1 can (1 pound 6 ounces) pineapple
pie filling
½ cup firm butter
1 package (14 ounces) orange muffin mix
1 cup flaked coconut
Vanilla ice cream

Heat oven to 400°. Pour pie filling into square pan, 9x9x2 inches. With pastry blender, cut butter into muffin mix (dry); stir in coconut. Sprinkle evenly over pie filling. Bake 35 to 40 minutes. Serve warm topped with ice cream.

*9 servings.*

# Index

Parfaits (cont.)
  chocolate, 57
    crunch, 57
  lemon, 57
Parker House rolls, 48
Parmesan
  French bread, 89
  veal, 81
  waffle fingers, 25
Parsleyed orange slices, 61
Party lamb chops, 49
Pea(s)
  and cabbage, buttered, 61
  and cauliflower, 32
  and lettuce, buttered, 61
  and potatoes, creamed, 63
  buttered green, and mushrooms, 103
  salad, tossed, 116
  tuna almondine with, 51
Peach(es)
  banana ambrosia, 66
  dessert, blushing, 105
  Riviera, 75
  shortcakes, jiffy, 116
  sparkling, 21
  sunny-side up, 50
  upside-down cake, 85
Peanut butter
  chocolate chip bars, 100
  chocolate sundaes, 19
  honey sundaes, 19
  'n jelly sundaes, 19
Peanut butterscotch sundaes, 19
Pear(s)
  au chocolat, 50
  cheese salad, 68
  gold rush salad, 71
Pecan-glazed apple pie, crunchy, 35
Pennsylvania Dutch salad, 35
Pepper steak, 78
Peppermint brownie rounds, 64
Peppers on the half shell, stuffed, 67
Pickled beets 'n onion rings, 25
Pie, apple
  crunchy pecan-glazed, 35
  lemon-glazed, 35
  orange-glazed, 35
Pineapple
  orange
    crunch, 122
    gel, quick, 73
  slices, broiled ham and, 17
  sparkling, 21
  tidbits with sherbet, 92
  tomato vinaigrette, 63
  upside-down cake, 85
Piquant sauce, 62
  liver with, 62
Pizza, mock, 37
Pizzaburger pie, 96
Poppy seed biscuits, 110

Pork
  chow mein, 72
  loin roast with savory gravy, 31
  'n stuffing bake, 86
  sparerib sauerkraut dinner, 106
  supper loaf, 44
Pork chop
  dinner-in-a-dish, 99
  scallop, 109
  skillet, orange, 102
Potato(es)
  and onions, broiled, 50
  creamed peas and, 63
  dogs, 65
  egg scramble, 23
  fish 'n chips, 20
  salad, hot German
    with bratwurst, 53
    with frankfurters, 53
  sweet, with banana, 19
Praline crunch sundaes, 68
Preparing ahead, 6

Q

Quantity make-ahead meatballs, 13
Quick
  chicken 'n dumplings, 34
  orange-pineapple gel, 73
Quickie bean salad, 66

R

Radish fans, 120
Raspberry delight, 98
Relish(es)
  cheese-stuffed celery and cherry tomatoes, 23
  crisp vegetable, 120
  kabobs, 38
  with cocktail sauce, 40
Rice
  browned, 73
  Spanish, mini meat loaves with, 76
  white, with chives, 73
Riviera peaches, 75
Roast
  pork loin, with savory gravy, 31
  turkey, orange-glazed, 29
Rolls
  baked frank, 37
  cloverleaf, 100
  grilled, 116
  Parker House, 48
  sesame, 80
Romanoff
  hamburger, 84
  meatballs, 39
  salmon, 60
Round steak, broiled, 46
  with mustard butter, 46
  with sesame butter, 46

S

Salad(s)
  cheese-stuffed celery and cherry tomatoes, 23
  cherry tomatoes and green onions, 16
  chived orange slices, 61
  combo fruit, 45
  cranberry-orange, 87
  creamy coleslaw, 103
  cucumber tomatoes, 55
  cucumbers in dilled sour cream, 21
  dilled cucumber, 32
  endive-lettuce, 98
  gold rush pear, 71
  golden ring, 71
  grapefruit-orange, 73
  hot cabbage slaw, 89
  lettuce
    and tomato, 94
    tomato towers, 100
    wedges with cucumber dressing, 26
    with croutons, 30
  mandarin, 80
  orange ambrosia slices, 61
  orange-onion, 83
    slices, 61
  parsleyed orange slices, 61
  pear cheese, 68
  Pennsylvania Dutch, 35
  pickled beets 'n onion rings, 25
  pineapple-tomato vinaigrette, 63
  potato, hot German
    with bratwurst, 53
    with frankfurters, 53
  quick orange-pineapple gel, 73
  quickie bean, 66
  stewed tomato, 52
  tomatoes vinaigrette, 85
  tossed
    avocado, 42
    fruit, 42
    green bean-mushroom, 57
    pea, 116
    wilted double green, 122
    zucchini, 75
Salmon Romanoff, 60
Sauerkraut
  sausage dinner, 108
  sparerib dinner, 106
Sausage sauerkraut dinner, 108
Sesame
  butter, broiled round steak with, 46
  butter sticks, 92
  cheese corn bread, 57
  rolls, 80
Sherbet
  melon balls and lemon, 92
  melon boats with, 92
  pineapple tidbits with, 92